40 Days with the Fathers

a daily reading plan

Luke J. Wilson

For more information or to contact the author, see:
www.thatancientfaith.uk

Dedicated to all those who love Jesus and His Church, and hold a deep appreciation of all those who have come before us, that great cloud of witnesses; and to my wife, Lucy, whose dedication to God has always been an inspiration.

Also dedicated to Dr David Allen (1940 - 2018) who brought Church History to life with his wit and humour and inspired my passion for the subject.

CONTENTS

PREFACE

This book originally took form on my blog[1] as a daily post throughout the period of Lent in 2017 (hence the 40 days), and aims to give you a glimpse into the minds of that great cloud of witnesses that have come before us to defend and uphold the faith.

While this book can be used as a Lenten reading plan, it still works well for any type of study or devotional time over a period of time, as these daily readings will really highlight the differing mindsets and issues which were around during the various points in the history of the Early Church and aren't dependant on it being Lent to be relevant. The various heresies and false teachers that plagued the early Christians are what many of these texts are defences against, as the authors aimed to establish sound doctrine, much of which we now take for granted.

The reading plan follows a collection of early texts from the first four centuries which comprises of a selection of extracts from various Early Church Fathers writings. For each day/chapter I give a short overview and any thoughts on the original text. This way, even if you don't read the corresponding texts you can still get a good idea of what each letter or "tome" is about. As an additional bit of information, at the beginning of each chapter I also include a preface which gives a *Who, What, Why* and *When* so you can read a short

1   That Ancient Faith — https://www.thatancientfaith.uk

summary about the historical context, purpose for it being written, and the approximate date of each ancient text as well. At the end of each chapter, there is a notes section so you can jot down any thoughts you had during your reading, and at the very end of the book are some useful appendices containing historical data and maps to help bring more visual context the the New Testament and Early Church texts.

Each daily reading should only take about 15 minutes of your time (though probably longer if you read the full texts alongside this book), and by day 40, you will have read ten different Church Fathers writings:

Didache, Diognetus, Polycarp, Ignatius, Justin Martyr, Cyprian, Athanasius, Cyril of Jerusalem, Ambrose of Milan, and Leo the Great.

You can read original texts online, or in the companion book which includes the full texts for each day/chapter (available to buy online).

I hope that you will enjoy this brief journey through the first 400 years of Church History from some of the more prominent Early Church leaders, Bishops and martyrs, and feel as challenged and enlightened about the Faith as I did after I first read these ancient witnesses.

INTRODUCTION

Why Read The Fathers?

Maybe for some of you reading this, the question might better be phrased as: *who are the Church Fathers?*

No doubt you will be familiar with some of their names: *Augustine, Jerome, Clement, Ignatius, Polycarp, Justin Martyr* et al. You may have even read portions or quotes by some of these men. But that still doesn't really explain to you *who* they are and *why* you should care, much less actually read any of their works.

This book deals with a selection of some of the most influential Early Church Fathers, sometimes also referred to as the Apostolic Fathers[2] (if they lived between AD 70-150), or the Ante Nicene Fathers for all of those in the period of time preceding the Council of Nicaea (AD 325). It is these men who wrote doctrine and defences against heresy and helped to continue and shape the Church in its most formative years.

Some of the earlier Christian leaders of the 2nd Century were discipled and taught by the Apostles

---

2   To read more of the Apostolic Fathers, I highly recommend: *The Apostolic Fathers, Greek and English translations, third edition;* Michael W. Holmes

themselves. Those include Clement of Rome,[3] Ignatius of Antioch and Polycarp of Smyrna. Still others in mid-2nd century were then taught by those who knew the men who were taught by some of the Apostles. One of the more well-known Bishops who was second generation to the Apostles was Irenaeus.[4]

From day (chapter) 21 onwards though, we look at a few writers from beyond this period (around 356) up until AD 449 where we can observe some distinctive changes in thought and practice.

These people who came before us, those great men of faith, many of whom suffered persecution and martyrdom to preserve the Church and Christ's mission, bridge the gap between the Bible and the present day. They fill the void we sometimes wonder about when we get to the end of reading Acts or the Epistles and think, *"what happened next?"* or *"what happened to the Ephesian church after Paul left?"*.

So Why Read What They Wrote?

The Bible didn't just drop out of the sky, all leather bound and ready to read for us to pick up today. There was a lengthy process of selecting and preserving the

---

3 Clement's epistle is not part of this book, but for reference, in 1 Clement 5:1-7 he speaks of the Apostles Peter and Paul as being of his "own generation" and holds them up as recent examples to follow. It is also one of the earliest extant Christian texts outside of the New Testament, alongside the Didache.

4 Irenaeus is best known for his extensive apologetic works, *Against Heresies*

apostles teachings which spanned nearly four centuries, and it was due to the Fathers and their faithfulness to the Scriptures that this was possible. Not only that, but due to their close links to the Apostles — some who were even taught directly by an apostle — we now have valuable resources and insights into aspects, teaching and issues within the very early Church which we can learn from and measure our doctrine and interpretation against.

This isn't to say that everything the Church Fathers said, did or wrote is perfect; or that we should elevate their texts to the level of Scripture, but we can glean much from those who knew and were discipled by the Apostles (or those who knew them second hand). We can read what certain portions of Scripture meant to them, or see how they interpreted things in the years following the Apostles, and can compare that to how we might read those same Scriptures today. This is a highly valuable resource for us to still have available; to be able to check our beliefs and doctrines against accepted, historical orthodoxy, which was quite literally shaped through blood, sweat and tears.

It's a wonderful thing to be able to look back millennia and know that what we believe and follow as Christians has been faithfully passed on and preserved for all this time.[5] Many doctrines we now take for granted were actually developed and defended during this time; carefully worded and formed to ensure that the truth of God doesn't get lost, diluted or warped for

---

5   *cf.* Jude 1:3

selfish gain.

We owe much to these men of God and can still learn a great deal from them, as they still speak to us today as part of that great cloud of witnesses who have gone before us.[6]

---

6 *cf.* Heb 12:1

DAY 1

THE DIDACHE

Who: Written by an anonymous author, possibly multiple sources compiled into one book at a later date. The title translates as "the teaching", or in its full title: *Teaching of the Twelve Apostles.*

What: The Didache is basically a church handbook with a summarised collection of the basic teachings of the Church and Gospel, aimed at local church leaders and new converts. It is one of the earliest examples of a written catechism that still exists, and it was also considered by some Early Church Fathers to be a part of the New Testament at one point, whereas others viewed it as spurious and it was eventually not canonised.

Why: Tradition has it as being a collection of the apostles teachings, so it was possibly written to preserve this information as they grew older or died, or moved away from the communities they planted.

When: Between 70-100 AD (possibly as early as 50 AD).

The Didache is one of my favourite extra-biblical books that I've read, so this is probably the fourth or fifth time I've been through it. I highly recommend taking the time to sit down and really digest it.

The book has 16 chapters, but don't let that put you off as they are pretty short and only about a couple of paragraphs each, since the whole point of this book is to be a quick overview or reference guide to various topics and doctrine within early Christianity. As you read through it, you'll find many familiar sayings and instructions from the New Testament, which makes sense if this is the contents of what the apostles continued to teach their new faith communities.

The book opens with a strong and definitive start: *The Two Ways*, one of *life* and one of *death:*

> The way of life, then, is this: First, you shall love God who made you; second, love your neighbour as yourself, and do not do to another what you would not want done to you

What follows is a list-style compilation summary of Jesus' teachings from the Gospel's, such as blessing those who curse you, and turning the other cheek etc.

The *way of death* and the "grave sin" which are forbidden, is reminiscent of the various lists of vices found in the Epistles which Paul writes to avoid if you want to enter the Kingdom of God.

Contrast what Paul wrote in 1 Corinthians 6:9-10 (and also in Galatians 5:19-21 and 1 Timothy 1:9-11) with the vice list that the Didache compiles:

1 Corinthians 6:9-10

Do you not know that wrongdoers will not inherit the kingdom of God? Do not be deceived! Fornicators, idolaters, adulterers, male prostitutes, sodomites, thieves, the greedy, drunkards, revilers, robbers — none of these will inherit the kingdom of God.

Galatians 5:19-21

Now the works of the flesh are obvious: fornication, impurity, licentiousness, idolatry, sorcery, enmities, strife, jealousy, anger, quarrels, dissensions, factions, envy, drunkenness, carousing, and things like these. I am warning you, as I warned you before: those who do such things will not inherit the kingdom of God.

1 Timothy 1:9-11

This means understanding that the law is laid down not for the innocent but for the lawless and disobedient, for the godless and sinful, for the unholy and profane, for those who kill their father or mother, for murderers, fornicators, sodomites, slave traders, liars, perjurers, and whatever else is contrary to the sound teaching that conforms to the glorious gospel of the blessed God, which he entrusted to me.

Didache 2

And the second commandment of the Teaching; You shall not commit murder, you shall not commit adultery, you shall not commit pederasty, you shall not commit fornication, you shall not steal, you shall not practice magic, you shall not practice witchcraft, you shall not murder a child by abortion nor kill that which is born. You shall not covet the things of your neighbour, you shall not swear, you shall not bear false witness, you shall not speak evil, you shall bear no grudge. You shall not be double-minded nor double-tongued, for to be double-tongued is a snare of death. Your speech shall not be false, nor empty, but fulfilled by deed. You shall not be covetous, nor rapacious, nor a hypocrite, nor evil disposed, nor haughty. You shall not take evil counsel against your neighbour.

Interestingly, in this list of sins which seem to be straight from the New Testament, there are a few modifications or additions. The two which stood out to me is that the Didache includes abortion as a sin (as well as killing children in general), and *pederasty.*[7]

That last sin, pederasty, links into what you may notice is "missing" from the Didache's list, but which seems to appear in Paul's list: homosexuality. Some New Testament's today translate Paul's words as *"men who have sex with men"* or *"those practising homosexuality"* (the NIV, for example, does this). The NRSV (quoted on the previous page) is a little less abrasive and says "male prostitutes", which at least gives some historical context; but there's still that ambiguous word "sodomite" in there.

The issue of translation comes from two underlying Greek words: *malakoi* and *arsenokoitai.* The latter, Paul coined himself, based off of the Septuagint

---

7   A word meaning: *'sexual activity involving a man and a boy'.*

translation of Leviticus 20:13 (*cf.* 18:22), so there's no straight-forward reference point for translation in contemporary texts.[8]

There isn't the space here to dwell too much on this area of translation or to go in depth on the Greek words, but there are various academic journals which have written extensively on the subject, with differing conclusions. See footnotes for some examples.[9] [10]

Here's where I believe the Didache actually helps to clarify this issue by not using the Greek word that Paul did, but rather has the word "Pederasty" (other translations say "[do not] corrupt children"[11]). Pederasty is defined as '*sexual activity involving a man and a boy'* which was a common practice amongst Romans.[12] The fact that this is included in such an early Christian document, written not that long after

---

8   Velotta, Jason R. "Who are the "Arsenokoitai" in 1 Co. 6:9?" *Academia.edu - Share research,* Mar. 2010, www.academia.edu/4984160/Who_are_the_Arsenokoitai_in_1_Co._6_9

9   Elliot, H. J. (2017, May 16) *No Kingdom of God for Softies? or, What Was Paul Really Saying? 1 Corinthians 6:9-10 in Context* Retrieved from https://www.researchgate.net/publication/254079554_No_Kingdom_of_God_for_Softies_or_What_Was_Paul_Really_Sayingquest_1_Corinthians_69-10_in_Context

10   De Young, James B. "The Source And NT Meaning Of Arsenokoitai, With Implications For Christian Ethics And Ministry" *The Master's Seminary,* 1992, https://www.tms.edu/m/tms-j3h.pdf.

11   Holmes, W. M., *The Apostolic Fathers* p.347

12   Williams, C. A., *Roman Homosexuality* p.23

Paul's letter to the Corinthians,[13] should shed some light on the early Christian understanding of the sexual sins which the Apostle was writing against.

Some of the other things that are quite striking about the Didache, are the practices described which demonstrate that certain doctrines the Church has taught throughout the centuries (via various denominations/branches) actually originated at the very start — well within the first century. Things such as baptism not always being full immersion, but sprinkling being permitted where water was scarce or not available to dunk in; and the gathering together on Sunday (the Lord's Day) to worship and break bread, along with various liturgy that has pretty much stayed the same. One thing which has fallen out of practice is the activity of praying the Lord's Prayer[14] three times a day and fasting every Wednesday and Friday (though this fasting practice still remains in the Eastern Orthodox Church and in some Catholic circles).

One of the things about baptism which I found particularly interesting is the instruction about "living water". We see this phrase used by Jesus in the Gospel

---

13 First Corinthians c. AD 53–54, Second Corinthians c. AD 55–56

14 Interesting side-note: When you recite the Lord's Prayer from memory, you likely finish it with *"...for yours is the power and glory forever, amen"* or similar. Now compare the Lord's Prayer in Matt 6:9-13 to the version in the Didache chapter eight and you'll see where we get our "extended version" from, probably without even realising that those last few words are not in the Gospel account.

of John in a spiritual sense[15] about the Holy Spirit, but in the Didache it is used just of regular water. Other translations[16] of this passage translate it simply as "running water" which I think helps to de-mystify some of the notions we have about what Jesus was saying.

There's also a great deal of information and teaching of how to recognise false prophets and apostles contrasted with true ones within a New Testament context, such as "If he asks for money, he is a false prophet". If we held the Didache as authoritative today, then chapters like this would deal a sharp blow to the "Prosperity Gospel" movement, I'm sure.

There was at one point in history, a time when this book was debated about being canonised and was considered to be part of the New Testament by some,[17] but it didn't make the cut in the end, possibly due to it being too broad or similar to the Gospels, or due to it's anonymous nature with no solid ties to Apostolic authorship[18] — but imagine the implications on Christianity if it had been, especially with its teaching on baptism, abortion and money-grabbing "prophets"!

---

15 *cf.* John 4:10-11; 7:37-38

16 Holmes, W. M., *The Apostolic Fathers* p.355

17 eg. Rufinus of Aquileia (344/345–411); John of Damascus (676–749) and the "broader canon" of the Ethiopian Orthodox Church (see: *http://www.ethiopianorthodox.org/english/canonical/books.html*)

18 eg. Eusebius considered it spurious but not heretical, and Athanasius excludes it from the canonical lists, but recommends it for reading (*cf.* 39th Paschal Letter)

I hope you enjoyed reading the Didache as much as I did, it really does pack a lot into such a short book! I would recommend reading the whole text in full as it offers so much insight into the teachings and doctrines of the very early Church, some of which can still inspire our faith today, or possibly even convict us if we have become slack — as some of the expectations on believers that the Didache places are quite high!

Let us examine our lives and walk with Christ in light of the *Two Ways* and made sure we live by the *Way of Life.*

Notes

Notes

DAY 2

EPISTLE OF MATHETES TO DIOGNETUS: CHAPS. 1–6

Who: Anonymous author, *"mathetes"* is not a name, but is the Greek word for "a disciple". Addressed to a certain Diognetus, who is otherwise unknown to us. There was a *Diognetus* who was a tutor of the emperor Marcus Aurelius, but he is not likely to be the actual recipient of this letter.[19]

What: Possibly one of the earliest examples of a Christian apologetic[20] defending the faith from its accusers, written to someone interested in learning more about the faith and its customs. Interestingly though, the term *Jesus* or *Christ* is not found in this letter at all, as the author seems to prefer the use of the term *"the Word"* instead.[21]

Why: The Christian faith was ridiculed and under attack in the early centuries, many things about the Church were misunderstood and so various Christians took to writing *apologetics* (defences) to clarify doctrines and prevent beliefs from being maligned.

When: Estimated between AD 130 and late 2nd century.

---

19 Grant, Robert M., *The Anchor Bible Dictionary, v. 2, p. 201*

20 A formal defence or justification of a theory or doctrine.

21 Kirby, Peter. "Epistle of Mathetes to Diognetus." Early Christian Writings. 2017. 19 Aug. 2017 <http://www.earlychristianwritings.com/diognetus.html>

This reading today is a particularly interesting one, as the author is contrasting the faith and practices of Christians against Greek and Jewish worship style and practice. Although, what I did find a little odd at first is how in this book (and others from the same time period), Jewish beliefs are often referred to as *"Jewish superstitions".*[22] In this context the author is referring to much of the traditional practices of the Jews that we'd recognise as being from the Torah. To us reading this today, that type of phrase may sound quite harsh, or disrespectful even, but it's a word that has changed its definition slightly over time.

In modern English, *superstition* is defined as "excessively credulous [or] irrational belief in supernatural influences",[23] whereas in ancient Latin usage, s*uperstitio* could mean the same as our modern understanding, but also an *"improper worship of the true God".* This is in contrast with the proper worship and awe of God (or the gods): *religio,* which is where we get our word "religion" from.[24]

So within this context, early Christian writers speaking of "Jewish superstition" were possibly referring to the fact that the Jews rejected Jesus as the

---

22 In AD 81, Roman emperor Domitian outlawed Christianity as a *superstitio Iudaica* — "Jewish superstition", as it was still considered a sect of Judaism at the time. *cf.* Shaheen, Y., *Rise and Fall of Gods: In Historical Perspective,* p. 105

23 Oxford Dictionary <https://en.oxforddictionaries.com/definition/superstition>

24 James 1:27 gives an example of how the word "religion" was used in a positive sense for right worship of God.

Messiah and thus were no longer worshipping God the Father in a proper manner any more.

The author goes into some depth of explaining the "vanity of idols" and how they are objects created by people and out of the materials we see and use everyday, and thus are no more special or worthy of honour. He invites Diognetus to contemplate "the substance and the form of those whom you declare and deem to be gods" because "[i]s not one of them a stone similar to that on which we tread?" — or brass, or wood, or silver, or iron. These so-called "gods" are no more divine than the material they are made from, and all can rot or rust or be stolen. Christians then, are hated on account of this because they "do not deem these [objects] to be gods" the author explains.

This then leads on to how Jewish worship, although correct due to it also rejecting idols, is still no better than the "example of madness" which Gentiles exhibit. This is because the Jews still observe similar things to the idol worship by offering "an act of folly than of divine worship" through their sacrifices to God, "supposing that they can give anything to Him who stands in need of nothing". This, in the authors mind, is no different than conferring "the same honour on things destitute of sense" and as such, all forms of Jewish worship — from observing the Sabbaths, to circumcision and new moons, are "utterly ridiculous and unworthy of notice", unlike the Christian practices which "abstain from the vanity and error common [to both Jews and Gentiles]".

This reading then finishes with a description of how Christians live and intermingle with society, yet are distinct from the world around them. I found this challenging and wondered if the description still applies to what we see today in the Church?

> [The Christians] display to us their wonderful and confessedly striking method of life. They dwell in their own countries, but simply as sojourners. As citizens, they share in all things with others, and yet endure all things as if foreigners. Every foreign land is to them as their native country, and every land of their birth as a land of strangers. They marry, as do all [others]; they beget children; but they do not destroy their offspring. They have a common table, but not a common bed. They are in the flesh, but they do not live after the flesh. They pass their days on earth, but they are citizens of heaven. They obey the prescribed laws, and at the same time surpass the laws by their lives. They love all men, and are persecuted by all. They are unknown and condemned; they are put to death, and restored to life. They are poor, yet make many rich; they are in lack of all things, and yet abound in all; they are dishonoured, and yet in their very dishonour are glorified. They are evil spoken of, and yet are justified; they are reviled, and bless; they are insulted, and repay the insult with honour; they do good, yet are punished as evil-doers. When punished, they rejoice as if quickened into life.

Notes

Notes

DAY 3

EPISTLE OF MATHETES TO DIOGNETUS: CHAPS. 7–12

Today's reading is the second, and final half of this letter to Diognetus. There's a lot more in these final chapters which focuses more on the glory and majesty of Christ and how he is the Lord and creator over all.

This is in contrast to the ancient Greeks who said that fire was a god, or water or various other elements (which means that anything could be a god to them), but the Christians recognise that *the Word* is creator *of* the elements, and is therefore greater and deserving of majesty and worship.

There is a lot of emphasis on "the Word" (*logos*) in these chapters and some great descriptions of the nature and love of God throughout the remaining portion of this book, but interestingly you don't see the name Jesus or the title of Christ in here at all — though there's no mistaking who the author is writing about.

One small detail which stood out to me near the end of the epistle, is when the author gives a small titbit of information about himself by saying that the things he is teaching are not "strange to [him]" nor is it "inconsistent with right reason" because he had been, in fact, "a disciple of the Apostles" and now had become "a teacher of the Gentiles"! The use of the title "the *Word*" throughout, and the high majestic descriptions of Jesus and the Father does have a striking resemblance to John's Gospel, but the themes of the letter also bear similarities to the tone of the Pauline epistles, so there's a possibility that this author may have been a disciple of John or Paul.[25]

Towards the end of this apologetic, an explanation is given as to why it took so long for Christ to come into the world, which gives us a good insight into the minds and views of early Christians as well as a very poetic description of the incarnation and atonement:

> But when our wickedness had reached its height, and it had been clearly shown that its reward, punishment and death, was impending over us; and when the time had come which God had before appointed for manifesting His own kindness and power, how the one love of God, through exceeding regard for men, did not regard us with hatred, nor thrust us away, nor remember our iniquity against us, but showed great long-suffering, and bore with us, He Himself took on Him the burden of our iniquities, He gave His own Son as a ransom for us, the holy One for transgressors, the blameless One for the wicked, the righteous One for the unrighteous, the incorruptible One for the corruptible, the immortal One for those who are mortal. For what other thing was capable of covering our sins than His righteousness?

> By what other one was it possible that we, the wicked and ungodly, could be justified, than by the only Son of God? O sweet exchange! O unsearchable operation! O benefits surpassing all expectation! That the wickedness of many should be hid in a single righteous One, and that the righteousness of One should justify many transgressors!

---

25 Introductory Note to the Epistle of Mathetes to Diognetus
 <https://www.ccel.org/ccel/schaff/anf01.iii.i.html>

There's one other thing which I'd like to pull out of today's reading (although there are many other things that could be said), and that's the continued description of Christians and their relation to the world in chapter seven. It opens by contrasting the nature and relation of the soul to the body as how Christians are to the world, in that while the flesh has its sinful desires at odds to the soul, the spiritual side pushes against that with love to overcome what is not of God.

I'll leave you with a quote of this portion, but I would highly recommend you give these six chapters a proper read as there is a lot packed into them!

> "To sum up all in one word--what the soul is in the body, that are Christians in the world. The soul is dispersed through all the members of the body, and Christians are scattered through all the cities of the world. The soul dwells in the body, yet is not of the body; and Christians dwell in the world, yet are not of the world. The invisible soul is guarded by the visible body, and Christians are known indeed to be in the world, but their godliness remains invisible. The flesh hates the soul, and wars against it, though itself suffering no injury, because it is prevented from enjoying pleasures; the world also hates the Christians, though in nowise injured, because they abjure pleasures. The soul loves the flesh that hates it, and [loves also] the members; Christians likewise love those that hate them."

Notes

DAY 4

EPISTLE OF POLYCARP: TO THE PHILIPPIANS

Who: Polycarp of Smyrna, who was a direct disciple of the apostle John. We also have some information about Polycarp via Irenaeus (who knew Polycarp) in his book, Against Heresies III, 3.4: "But Polycarp also was not only instructed by apostles, and conversed with many who had seen Christ, but was also, by apostles in Asia, appointed bishop of the Church in Smyrna".

What: This letter contains many exhortations to the Philippian church by Polycarp. This epistle is also referenced by Irenaeus in one of his letters as recommended reading for those who "are anxious about their salvation" so that they "can learn the character of [Polycarp's] faith, and the preaching of the truth" from him.

Why: Much like the New Testament letter to the Philippians, it it written to encourage the church on its faith and perseverance of salvation.

When: Estimated 110-140 AD[26]

---

26 Biblical scholars generally agree that Paul wrote his epistle to the Philippians around 62 AD.

One of the first things that will strike you about this letter is that if you didn't know any better, you'd think it was a Pauline epistle you were reading!

It has all the trappings of a classic New Testament pastoral letter to a local church, from the way it opens with the typical greetings and salutations, to the way it closes with praise and recommendations of other believers.

This letter is all about encouraging and urging the church in Philippi to continue to stay strong in the faith delivered to them, since they had a "strong root of … faith, spoken of in days long gone by" — which is a direct reference to Paul's letter and encouragement, found in Philippians 1:3-6.

There's so many references to other New Testament letters in here, that you can find at least one reference to nearly all of the canonised books, plus a couple of Old Testament quotes, including one from Tobit.[27] This in itself gives a small insight to what books were being considered as authoritative within the Church communities during this early period.

Polycarp does mention the "blessed and glorified Paul" in his letter, and gives him his dues so as not to appear to be stepping on toes, with a short summary of Paul's original letter to this church and it's purpose:

---

27 The Book of Tobit is a part of the Catholic and Orthodox biblical canon, but not included in the Protestant canon.

> He (Paul), when among you, accurately and steadfastly taught the word of truth in the presence of those who were then alive. And when absent from you, he wrote you a letter, which, if you carefully study, you will find to be the means of building you up in that faith which has been given you

I just like seeing things like this in these other texts, where the apostles get a little 'shout-out', as I think it just draws home the reality of the New Testament narratives and that these were real people in real communities who were being impacted by the power of the Gospel.

There's also some warnings and harsh words against those who teach Docetism[28] — Polycarp calls those false teachers the "firstborn of Satan", quoting 1 John 4; and he also expresses that he is "deeply grieved" for one of the church leaders whom he knew who had fallen into sin, and stresses that the church should avoid similar sin and call him back to repentance in love.

In light of this, Polycarp urges the church to remember the teaching they received "which has been handed down to [them] from the beginning", and to return to those principles they were taught:

> …"watching unto prayer",[29] and persevering in fasting;

---

28 The false teaching and belief that Jesus' humanity was an illusion.

29 *cf.* 1 Peter 4:7

beseeching in our supplications the all-seeing God "not to lead us into temptation",[30] as the Lord has said: "The spirit truly is willing, but the flesh is weak."[31]

Along with this letter, Polycarp also included all of Ignatius' epistles, which were highly commended to be read and passed on amongst the churches.

Overall, this letter feels very familiar and is just as encouraging as the Pauline letters we read in the New Testament, which is unsurprising in some ways since Polycarp knew, and was discipled by the Apostle John, and met with many others who had seen and known Jesus, and so possibly picked up on certain teaching and writing styles.

Polycarp is regarded as a link to the Apostolic era due to his association with John and others who knew Jesus, with his witness being highly regarded as he could testify to the genuine tradition of apostolic teaching and doctrine against that of the heretical teachers who were cropping up. This letter is definitely well worth at least one complete read through in order to fully appreciate it and see why it was a popular and important epistle which was circulated amongst the early churches.

---

30 *cf.* Matthew 6:13; Matthew 26:41

31 *cf.* Matthew 26:41; Mark 14:38

Notes

Notes

DAY 5

IGNATIUS OF ANTIOCH: LETTER TO THE EPHESIANS

Who: Ignatius converted at a young age and later became Bishop of Antioch. A friend of Polycarp and fellow disciple of John, there is a long standing tradition that Ignatius was the child that Jesus held in his arms and blessed in Mark 10:13-16

What: The letter has a strong call to and for unity within the church, along with respect for their bishop.

Why: Ignatius wrote a series of letters to the churches in Asia Minor whilst en route to Rome to face martyrdom by wild beasts in the Colosseum around 108 AD.

When: Around 107-108 AD

This is the third letter we have which was sent to the church in Ephesus. Other than Paul's letter to the Ephesian church, there was one other which is briefly mentioned in Revelation 2:1-7 as one of the seven churches in Asia to which Jesus sends a message to via John. The church was commended then for its perseverance and vigilance against false apostles and teachers, a virtue which appears to have been kept until Ignatius' time.

From the outset, there is a strong theme to this letter about having unity in the faith, something which Ignatius stresses. He repeatedly calls for this unity and commends the Ephesian church on it, especially for the fact that no sects have cropped up from within. Ignatius is also very pleased that the whole congregation came to visit him whilst en route to be executed — something which he was apparently looking forward to, *"so by martyrdom [he] may indeed become the disciple of [Jesus]"*!

Ignatius also has a lot of respect for Onesimus,[32] bishop of this church in Ephesus, and really sings his praises throughout the first few chapters. The man sounds quite something, but I especially liked this imagery that Ignatius uses to describe how well suited this man is for the position of bishop, "like strings to a harp" which makes the rest of the church sing in unity:

For your justly renowned presbytery, worthy of God, is

---

32 Possibly the same Onesimus mentioned by Paul in Colossians 4:9 and Philemon 1:8-10, though scholarship and tradition differ on this.

fitted as exactly to the bishop as the strings are to the harp. Therefore in your concord and harmonious love, Jesus Christ is sung.

Chapter six has warnings against false teachers, which, by the statement about Christ's nature that follows, would seem to be combating Docetism like Polycarp's letter also did. But whereas Polycarp referenced 1 John 4 as a defence, Ignatius gives us an early glimpse of the view of Christ's deity and dual nature:

> There is one Physician who is possessed both of flesh and spirit; both made and not made; God existing in flesh; true life in death; both of Mary and of God; first passible and then impassible, even Jesus Christ our Lord ... God Himself being manifested in human form for the renewal of eternal life.

Considering the date of this letter, this in itself is a good apologetic against the more recent false claims that Jesus was only "made" divine at the Council of Nicaea, when the gathered bishops and Emperor Constantine "decided" to alter centuries of Church doctrine and make Jesus into more than he supposedly was.[33] This is, of course, total nonsense and even a cursory reading of Church History and the documents *from* the Council would dispel this notion, but the internet being what it is makes these heresies survive. But I digress.

---

33 This modern heresy is perpetrated by a group called the *Hebrew Roots Movement,* which goes as far as denying the Trinity, deity of Christ and enforces the Law on its followers.

Towards the end of the letter, Ignatius also gives us an overview of the gospel, and from what I understand, one of the earliest extra-biblical accounts for the virgin birth:[34]

> For our God, Jesus Christ, was, according to the appointment of God, conceived in the womb by Mary, of the seed of David, but by the Holy Ghost.

Along with more calls and praises for unity, Ignatius seems to have very clear views on Church structure and hierarchy in regards to obeying the presbyters and deacons, and imitating them as they imitate Christ; along with a similar encouragement found in Hebrews[35] to meet regularly together in the same place because, as he says, *"the powers of Satan are destroyed ... by the unity of your faith"*.

The insight on Communion (or the Eucharist) which this letter gives us, is also quite interesting as Ignatius writes that the breaking of bread *"is the medicine of immortality, and the antidote to prevent us from dying"* which will enable us to *"live forever in Jesus Christ"*.

It's a very interesting letter, with some unique insights into the theology of the early church and the

---

34 The very fact that Ignatius mentions this without any further explanation, along with the date of this letter, is a great witness and testimony in itself to the doctrine being accepted within the Church long before this letter was penned.

35 *cf.* Hebrews 10:25

importance of unity amongst the believers. There is a lot of repetition though, where Ignatius really labours his point about unity. But in the face of persecution, heresy and false teachers trying to infiltrate and cause divisions in the church, it's understandable why he would get passionate about those within this congregation standing strong and together in the faith.

May we also have this same passion for our fellow brothers and sisters in Christ.

Notes

DAY 6

IGNATIUS OF ANTIOCH: LETTER TO THE MAGNESIANS

Who: Ignatius converted at a young age and later became Bishop of Antioch. A friend of Polycarp and fellow disciple of John, there is a long standing tradition that Ignatius was the child that Jesus held in his arms and blessed in Mark 10:13-16

What: Ignatius urges the church in Magnesia, Greece, to continue in unity, to honour their leadership and to avoid Judaizers who may try to bring false teaching. This letter also gives some valuable insight to early church hierarchy.

Why: Ignatius wrote a series of letters to the churches in Asia Minor whilst en route to Rome to face martyrdom by wild beasts in the Colosseum around 108 AD.

When: Around 107-108 AD

Today continues with Ignatius' next letter which he wrote on his travels through Asia Minor towards his martyrdom. This letter goes to the Magnesian church, which he highly commended for their faith.

There is definitely a strong theme with regards to the structure of church leadership and how the believers should trust and follow their bishops — similar to Ignatius' other letters, but now it begins to make more sense in this letter as his thinking on the matter is displayed more clearly. He urges the church to submit to their bishop because in doing so, they are in fact submitting to the Father, who is "bishop of us all".

The opening chapters of this letter reminded me of Paul when he wrote to Timothy to encourage him in his position within the church, despite his youth.[36] In a similar manner, Ignatius is advising this church in Magnesia to not become too familiar with their bishop "on account of his youth", but to remember his position as a leader of the church and so to "yield him all reverence".

Chapter six actually gives us a really good insight into the theology behind church hierarchy, and why Ignatius is emphasising obeying the bishop and presbyters so much — they are essentially the representation of God and the Apostles to the congregation! Look at how Ignatius puts it:

...your bishop presides in the place of God, and your

---

36 *cf.* 1 Tim 4:12

> presbyters in the place of the assembly of the apostles, along with your deacons, who are most dear to me, and are entrusted with the ministry of Jesus Christ

That's some high standards to live up to. It's no wonder the qualifications for these positions were strict if this was the thinking behind them. Maybe this was the thought even when Paul first penned his letters to Timothy and Titus about leadership qualifications?[37]

It's also because of this understanding that Ignatius instructs the congregation to not do anything "without the bishop and presbyters" since, as Jesus did nothing without the Father, and the Apostles without Jesus, so neither should the Church without their leadership. It's interesting to see that this church structure was active from so early on, and not something created hundreds of years after the fact.

The final chapters warn against "strange doctrines" and "old fables", which mainly seems to be about Judaizers who would teach the new believers to follow the old ways of Judaism. This would be another early example of the views of the Church in regards to the Jewish Law and how it relates to Christians, "For if we still live according to the Jewish law," Ignatius says, "we acknowledge that we have not received grace", which you can see is a statement echoing Paul's sentiments throughout his letters to the churches — *"you are not under law, but under grace"* as he wrote

---

37 *cf.* 1 Tim 3:1-7; 8-13; Tit 1:5-9

in Romans 6:14.[38]

This whole chapter is pretty much a short summary of Paul's teaching on the Law and how we Christians are no longer bound by it. *"You who want to be justified by the law have cut yourselves off from Christ; you have fallen away from grace"*,[39] as Paul wrote — or as Ignatius phrases it, "it is absurd to profess Christ Jesus, and to Judaize". The message is consistent, Christians are no longer under the Law of Moses, but "have come to the possession of a new hope, no longer observing the Sabbath, but living in the observance of the Lord's Day".

An encouraging letter to read, offering some valuable insight to the early church and their understanding of our relation to the Law as Christians.

---

38 *cf.* Rom 7:4,6; Gal 4:21 etc.

39 *cf.* Gal 5:4

Notes

Notes

DAY 7

IGNATIUS OF ANTIOCH: LETTER TO THE TRALLIANS

Who: Ignatius converted at a young age and later became Bishop of Antioch. A friend of Polycarp and fellow disciple of John, there is a long standing tradition that Ignatius was the child that Jesus held in his arms and blessed in Mark 10:13-16

What: Ignatius urges the church to continue in unity and to honour their leadership. This letter also gives a defence against certain heresies.

Why: Ignatius wrote a series of letters to the churches in Asia Minor whilst en route to Rome to face martyrdom by wild beasts in the Colosseum around 108 AD.

When: Around 107-108 AD

The letter to the Trallians is shorter than the previous two by Ignatius we've read so far. But much like the others, there's a lot said for keeping in unity in Christ and for following their bishop and presbyters, and not to do anything apart from their instruction. Ignatius makes reference to his impending death again for the sake of the Gospel, and in doing so leads into a defence against Docetism, again.

This heresy, or that of Judaizers, comes up in every letter, which goes to show that even this early on, Christians were really up against it all having to defend the truth of the Gospel from every direction.

Because of the nature of the Docetic beliefs — that Jesus wasn't really manifest in the flesh but was rather an illusion, Ignatius gives us a nice run down of the life and passion of Jesus, which really focusses on his physical nature.

Like John wrote so clearly in his Gospel: *"the Word became flesh"*,[40] Ignatius writes a similar summary of the Gospel message in order to combat any notions that Christ was anything but human in manifestation.

There appeared to be those who taught "that [Jesus] only seemed to suffer" and if that were so, Ignatius argued, "then why am I in bonds … Do I therefore die in vain? Am I not then guilty of falsehood against [the cross of] the Lord?".

We don't see much of this heresy around today,

40 *cf.* John 1:14

though it has its forms here and there (such as within Islam[41]), but it's not such a great threat to the Faith now as it used to be. Even so, remembering the fact that Jesus was indeed "revealed in flesh, vindicated in spirit, seen by angels, proclaimed among Gentiles, believed in throughout the world, [and] taken up in glory"[42] — this is the cornerstone of our faith. Anything less is not the Gospel, and that is what Ignatius was emphasising to this church.

I'm going to close by quoting Ignatius' "history of Christ" because I really like the way it summarises the Gospel and emphasises the reality and physicality of it all:

> Stop your ears, therefore, when anyone speaks to you at variance with Jesus Christ, who was descended from David, and was also of Mary; who was truly born, and did eat and drink. He was truly persecuted under Pontius Pilate; He was truly crucified, and [truly] died, in the sight of beings in heaven, and on earth, and under the earth. He was also truly raised from the dead, His Father quickening Him, even as after the same manner His Father will so raise up us who believe in Him by Christ Jesus, apart from whom we do not possess the true life.

Though the Docetic heresy may not be prominent today, does a form of it dwindle in your thoughts? Has the reality of the Gospel really taken root in your heart

---

41 *cf.* Quran, Surah An-Nisa 4:157 <https://quran.com/4/157>

42 *cf.* 1 Tim 3:16

and mind? Meditate on the reality of the Gospel message and on Jesus — his incarnation and manifestation in this world 2000 years ago — and consider the reality of his Spirit now dwelling in you today.[43] Let that really take a hold of you as you go about your day.

---

43 *cf.* Romans 8:9

Notes

Notes

DAY 8

IGNATIUS OF ANTIOCH: LETTER TO THE ROMANS

Who: Ignatius converted at a young age and later became Bishop of Antioch. A friend of Polycarp and fellow disciple of John, there is a long standing tradition that Ignatius was the child that Jesus held in his arms and blessed in Mark 10:13-16

What: A challenging letter in which Ignatius pours himself out to the Roman church about his impending martyrdom.

Why: Ignatius wrote a series of letters to the churches in Asia Minor whilst en route to Rome to face martyrdom by wild beasts in the Colosseum around 108 AD.

When: Around 107-108 AD

On reading the introduction to this letter, my first thought was *"wow!"* because Ignatius *really* liked this Roman church. The opening paragraph is literally a string of praises that they are worthy of, for example: *"worthy of God, worthy of honour, worthy of the highest happiness, worthy of praise, worthy of obtaining her every desire, worthy of being deemed holy"*. This is very different to the previous letters, in which he highly praised the bishops as well as the faith of the previous churches, but there has be nothing quite like this so far.

In all of Ignatius' letters so far, he has mentioned that he is bound as a prisoner for Christ, on his way to face beasts and that in doing so he will "attain to God" and truly become a disciple of Jesus through martyrdom. But this time it's different. He actually pleads with the Roman church not to do anything that will prevent his death!

From the way he writes, it sounds like the church in Rome had great influence and could have probably changed his sentence to have Ignatius set free. But he writes to them saying that he is "afraid" of their love, "lest it should do me an injury" because it was easy for the Roman church to "accomplish what [they] please" which, in his mind, would make it difficult for him to "attain to God" if they show their love to his flesh and thus cause him to have to run his race once again from the start.

This letter is overall different in its tone and I found the things Ignatius said quite a challenge.

Ignatius repeatedly says he will "willingly die for God" and to let him "become food for the wild beasts" because he is "the wheat of God", to be "ground by the teeth of the wild beasts", so that he "may be found the pure bread of God" and that the wild beasts "may become [his] tomb".

He is really living out the truth of the Gospel of willingly laying down his life for God, even in the face of a horrendous death by wild animals! It reminds me of one of my favourite Scriptures, a similar situation actually, when Paul is bound and on his way to Jerusalem to face death and he says:

Acts 20:24
But I do not count my life of any value to myself, if only I may finish my course and the ministry that I received from the Lord Jesus, to testify to the good news of God's grace.

This right here sums up everything Ignatius is saying and desires. His resolve is steadfast, even with the opportunity to get out of this situation via help from the Roman church. I wonder how many of us, myself included, would have such strength of faith in the face of certain death — especially a death like this?

As Ignatius said, he wants to "not merely be called a Christian, but really found to be one" through his actions and outward faith, whatever the circumstances. He does give us a small insight into what drives him during this time, because not only is he facing execution, but has ten soldiers guarding him who are not exactly treating him well, by the sounds of things. But despite this, he tells us that, "there is within me a water that liveth and speaketh, saying to me inwardly, Come to the Father". The Spirit drives him and comforts him, and in this he draws his strength to face whatever comes.

> Now I begin to be a disciple. And let no one, of things visible or invisible, envy me that I should attain to Jesus Christ. Let fire and the cross; let the crowds of wild beasts; let tearings, breakings, and dislocations of bones; let cutting off of members; let shatterings of the whole body; and let all the dreadful torments of the devil come upon me: only let me attain to Jesus Christ.

I began this letter wowed, but leave it feeling a bit stunned. It kind of puts things into perspective, in that we in the West really have it quite easy these days as Christians. The challenges we face today are vastly different from these early Christians (and, indeed, believers in other parts of the world today), but the freedom we have is something which I don't think we always appreciate as much as we could.

May we find strength and comfort in Christ by the power of the Spirit, to face whatever challenges come our way in life, even unto death. *Amen.*

Notes

Notes

DAY 9

IGNATIUS OF ANTIOCH: LETTER TO THE PHILADELPHIANS

Who: Ignatius converted at a young age and later became Bishop of Antioch. A friend of Polycarp and fellow disciple of John, there is a long standing tradition that Ignatius was the child that Jesus held in his arms and blessed in Mark 10:13-16

What: As usual, a general call to remain in unity and heed their bishop. Also to avoid listening to Judaizers who would have them follow the Law.

Why: Ignatius wrote a series of letters to the churches in Asia Minor whilst en route to Rome to face martyrdom by wild beasts in the Colosseum around 108 AD.

When: Around 107-108 AD

As with the rest of Ignatius' letters, there is the message of unity stressed throughout this, along with the call to heed their bishop's teaching and leadership.

As to this point, Ignatius recalls to the Philadelphians a time when he was among them as a speaker. He reminds them what he taught, making the point that what he said came to him by the Spirit and was not "intelligence from any man":

> But the Spirit proclaimed these words: Do nothing without the bishop; keep your bodies as the temples of God; love unity; avoid divisions; be the followers of Jesus Christ, even as He is of His Father.

Ignatius emphasised the role of the Spirit here because there were apparently those who were trying to cause division, and this message he brought spoke right into the heart of that situation, presumably dissolving the situation before it got out of hand, and putting the fear of God in them. I find it interesting that Ignatius repeats mostly what Paul teaches, except with the added instruction to follow the bishop explicitly — which was apparently said to him by the Spirit.

This in itself shows us the importance of listening to the Spirit for our guidance in all situations, and is a good example of the outworking of what Jesus promised his followers when he said not to worry about what you'll say because the Spirit will give to the words.[44]

---

44 *cf.* Jn 16:13; Mk 13:11

Like in his letter to the Magnesians, Ignatius again highlights the importance of avoiding Judaizers. "If any one preach the Jewish law unto you, listen not to him" he urges, because if they do, Ignatius says, they are no better than "monuments and sepulchres of the dead" since they preach that which has passed away.

He goes on to contrast the Old Testament with the New by saying that, "the priests indeed are good, but the High Priest is better" because "He is the door of the Father, by which enter in Abraham, and Isaac, and Jacob, and the prophets, and the apostles, and the Church". Christ is now the way, and only way, to God the Father, and as such the old ways of Judaism are no longer in effect.

He emphasises this even more by pointing out that, "the Gospel possesses something transcendent [above the former dispensation]" and that is: "the appearance of our Lord Jesus Christ" along with his death and resurrection.

The "prophets announced Him, but the Gospel is the perfection of immortality" and so, why would we need anything more? Judaism pointed the way to the Gospel and to the Messiah, but now that his appearance has been made known, the old is superseded by the new. As the writer of Hebrews says;

Hebrews 8:13
In speaking of "a new covenant," he has made the first one obsolete. And what is obsolete and growing old will soon disappear.

This was written whilst the temple still stood and animal sacrifices were still being made, and so the old was still fading and disappearing.[45]

But now in Ignatius' time it has been about 30 years since the destruction of Jerusalem and the temple, so the old really had disappeared and as far as he was concerned, the New Covenant was in full effect which is why his letters often remind the churches not to fall back into the old ways of Judaism.

That is something that I think many Christians today still need reminding of as well. We have been set free in Christ,[46] taken out from under the power of the old and are now under a new Law: *the Law of Love/Christ*.[47]

Go, therefore, in freedom.

---

45 *cf.* Heb 9:8-9

46 *cf.* Acts 13:39; Rom 8:2; Rom 10:4; Gal 5:1

47 *cf.* Rom 13:10; Gal 5:14; Gal 6:2

Notes

Notes

DAY 10

IGNATIUS OF ANTIOCH: LETTER TO THE SMYRNAEANS

Who: Ignatius converted at a young age and later became Bishop of Antioch. A friend of Polycarp and fellow disciple of John, there is a long standing tradition that Ignatius was the child that Jesus held in his arms and blessed in Mark 10:13-16

What: A defence against the heresy of Docetism and an intriguing insight into the possible origins of evil spirits.

Why: Ignatius wrote a series of letters to the churches in Asia Minor whilst en route to Rome to face martyrdom by wild beasts in the Colosseum around 108 AD.

When: Around 107-108 AD

The opening chapters of this letter pulls no punches in regards to the heresy of Docetism. Ignatius commends this church for "being fully persuaded" in the truth of Christ — that he was born of a virgin, was baptised and truly did suffer and die on the cross for us; not, as some were saying, that "He only seemed to suffer". To these, Ignatius says that they "only seem to be [Christians]" because of their false teaching!

He defends the resurrection by telling of how the Apostles ate and drank with, and touched the risen Christ since "He was still possessed of flesh", but to this he also adds that he believes Jesus is *still* possessing a body of flesh, whilst being spiritually "united to the Father". I'm not sure if he means this in the same way we might today when we talk about the glorified/resurrected bodies, since you don't often hear people say they are "flesh" in the physical, human sense, but it's likely just a semantics issue here.

With regards to the unbelievers who taught that Jesus wasn't really in the flesh, Ignatius gives us a strange insight into a belief about where evil spirits come from. Because they teach that Jesus only seemed to have a real body after his resurrection, so these people will also only seem to as well; they will essentially reap what they sow and "shall be divested of their bodies, and be mere evil spirits"! That is definitely an intriguing insight, but I'm not sure how common this belief was in the Early Church, or whether this is actually the implication that Ignatius meant.

But there is still hope for these people, and by extension, any today who preach heresy. Stay away from them, Ignatius says, and only pray to God for these people so that they may be brought to repentance, although this "will be very difficult", but Jesus has the power to make this happen if he wills.

Following on from this there is a comment about this belief in regards to the Eucharist and how these unbelievers say that it is not "the flesh of our Saviour Jesus Christ" — an early reference to the doctrine of the Real Presence[48] or maybe transubstantiation[49]? Either way, the heretics taught that the bread and wine were *not* the flesh and blood and were condemned for it, which obviously has implications on those today who hold these to be merely symbols — if there's any weight to Ignatius' words or to early doctrine. It's something to ponder on at the very least.

The closing chapters are similar to the other letters: they praise the bishop (his friend Polycarp, in this instance) and the church for their faith; and also for being steadfast against the heresies which Ignatius condemns. Whilst the previous letters all say the same thing about listening to the bishop and to not do anything apart from him, this letter goes one further and says that *"he who does anything without the knowledge of the bishop, does [in reality] serve the devil"!*

---

48 The doctrine that Jesus is really or substantially present in the Eucharist, and not only symbolically or metaphorically

49 The Roman Catholic doctrine that the bread and wine actually become the literal body and blood of Christ

That's some strong words there and it really shows the emphasis on the church hierarchy in these early days, as well as the serious positions of these church leaders — as though they were acting in place of Jesus and the Apostles to the individual churches — which is often how Ignatius describes it.

Like the others, this letter of Ignatius gives us a possible glimpse of where certain doctrines had their origins, and it really offers some interesting viewpoints to think about that could potentially challenge your own beliefs.

Notes

Notes

DAY 11

IGNATIUS OF ANTIOCH: LETTER TO POLYCARP

Who: Ignatius converted at a young age and later became Bishop of Antioch. A friend of Polycarp and fellow disciple of John, there is a long standing tradition that Ignatius was the child that Jesus held in his arms and blessed in Mark 10:13-16

What: A letter addressed personally to Polycarp giving him advice and encouragement as a bishop, plus some instructions on marriage for the church, which are reminiscent of Paul's epistles.

Why: Ignatius wrote a series of letters to the churches in Asia Minor whilst en route to Rome to face martyrdom by wild beasts in the Colosseum around 108 AD.

When: Around 107-108 AD

This is the final letter by Ignatius, and it ends with him writing personally to his fellow bishop Polycarp, bishop of Smyrna (modern day Izmir, Turkey) who was the leader of the church in which yesterday's reading was addressed to. Whereas the previous letters were all written to the church as a whole, with praise and exhortations of their bishops, this one is addressed directly to a bishop personally.

Ignatius aims to encourage Polycarp in this letter by acknowledging his strengths and steadfast faith, and also by reminding him off his duties and role as a bishop. There's a brief warning against "those who seem worthy of credit", but actually "teach strange doctrines" which may fill Polycarp with some "apprehension".

This warning would seem to be against Docetism again, as in all of Ignatius' previous letters, which leads him to write this short creed about Christ just to reiterate the Church's stance on the matter, and although it's only short, I do like it, especially the parallelism:

> Look for Him who is above all time, eternal and invisible, yet who became visible for our sakes; impalpable and impassible, yet who became passible on our account; and who in every kind of way suffered for our sakes.

What follows this are a few instructions, or advice maybe, to Polycarp, which isn't too unusual since

Ignatius is the elder of the two bishops — probably well into his 70s by this point, Polycarp maybe in his 40s. We see the inverse of what the previous letters have encouraged the church body to do (*"do nothing without the bishop"*) where here we see that same advice given to Polycarp but from a leadership point of view. "Let nothing be done without thy consent" he is told, but also not to do "anything without the approval of God". The position of bishop was not one to be abused or taken lightly, and those who held that office were to be subject to God and to the leading of the Spirit all the more.

Polycarp is encouraged to "flee evil arts" — or *"wicked practices"* as other translations have it — but to also make sure that he preaches against such things in public. Within the rest of this chapter, there is a quick run down of instructions concerning marriage and how to pastor those who want to be married, or who already are.

There are similar calls to marriage purity and relationships as Paul gives in Eph 5:25, which is likely what Ignatius had in mind when he wrote that Polycarp should encourage the men to "love their wives, even as the Lord the Church", but also to those who are unmarried and virgins, they should strive to remain "in a state of purity" — another echo of Paul's teaching on marriage in 1 Cor 7:8.

But there is a definite change of thinking between what Paul wrote and what Ignatius says to Polycarp in the remainder of this chapter. Where Paul says that "it is better to marry than to be aflame with passion"[50] with no other rules attached, Ignatius writes saying that those who wish to marry should plan to "form their union with the approval of the bishop" so that it may be a Godly coupling and not something formed "after their own lust".

For all of times that Ignatius quotes Paul in his letters, it seems strange now that there has been a subtle change with regards to marriage which departs slightly from Paul's instruction. Maybe this is a rule formed from the inference in what Paul says in 1 Cor 7 about widows who want to marry again, but "only in the Lord", i.e. to other believers; or more explicitly, from 2 Cor 6:14 where he instructs that believers should not be "unequally yoked" (or "mismatched") with unbelievers. But even when taking this into consideration, requiring permission from the bishop is a new one.

After this there is a shift of audience in the letter as it appears to go from talking personally to Polycarp, to speaking to the whole congregation. "Give ye heed to the bishop" chapter six begins, speaking of Polycarp in the third person, and not by name. What follows is a familiar call to live in unity with one another, but said in words which are reminiscent once again of Paul:

> Labour together with one another; strive in company together; run together; suffer together; sleep together; and awake together, as the stewards, and associates, and servants of God. Please ye Him under whom ye

---

50 *cf.* 1 Cor 7:9

fight, and from whom ye receive your wages. Let none of you be found a deserter. Let your baptism endure as your arms; your faith as your helmet; your love as your spear; your patience as a complete panoply. Let your works be the charge assigned to you, that ye may receive a worthy recompense. Be long-suffering, therefore, with one another, in meekness, as God is towards you.

I don't know about you, but when reading this excerpt I can almost feel the desire which Ignatius had towards his fellow churches and his passion to see everyone live out that goal to have "love for one another", which Jesus prayed for, so that "everyone will know that you are [Jesus'] disciples".[51]

The closing chapters display more of this unity of the churches being lived out as there are instructions to send various letters and messengers between the churches far and wide where Ignatius won't be able to make it to, so that the message and teaching may be consistent.

This is the final letter of Ignatius due to him being martyred shortly after by wild animals in Rome. There is another letter called "The Martyrdom of Ignatius" which isn't included here, but you can read it in full in the appendix of the companion book to this reading plan.

Since I've mentioned it though, here's a short

---

51 *cf.* Jn 13:35

overview on the aforementioned epistle: Scholarly opinion is somewhat divided on the authenticity of *The Martyrdom* epistle, with some accepting it as totally genuine, others partially and some rejecting it completely. You can read a brief overview on this subject online.[52]

In brief though, if it is genuine, the letter is supposed to written by those who accompanied Ignatius on his travels through Asia Minor and who also witnessed his execution in Rome. After a lengthy trip, they eventually landed in Rome where Ignatius "was thus cast to the wild beasts". The believers in the city "spent the whole night in tears" and prayer to the Lord, and it is recorded in the closing chapter of this letter that some "saw the blessed Ignatius" after his death standing with them and embracing the group, and "others beheld him again praying" for them and lastly, some saw him sweating and "standing by the Lord" as though coming from "his great labour".

Whether you accept the genuineness of this last letter or not, I think it gives some nice closure to the life of Ignatius which we've briefly been following over the last few days.

---

52 *cf.* Introductory Note to the Martyrdom of Ignatius: *http://www.biblestudytools.com/history/early-church-fathers/ante-nicene/vol-1-apostolic-with-justin-martyr-iren-aeus/ignatius/introductory-note-martyrdom-of-ignatius.html*

Notes

Notes

DAY 12

JUSTIN MARTYR: FIRST APOLOGY, CHAPS. 1-11

Who: Born in Samaria, Justin Martyr was a philosopher who came to Christianity around 130 AD. He lived out the last part of his life in Rome where he was martyred by beheading around 165 AD.

What: A compelling defence (*apologetic*) of the faith written to the Roman emperor, Antoninus Pius[53] and his adopted sons.

Why: Justin is demanding that the Emperor to investigate accusations and unjust persecution against Christians so that they may at least face a fair trial. It is also believed that *First Apology* was possibly written in response to Polycarp's martyrdom. He was burned alive at the stake in Rome in the same year Justin wrote this essay.[54]

When: Around 156 AD

---

53 Roman emperor from AD 138 to 161

54 Grant, Robert, *Greek Apologists of the Second Century* (1988)

Here we begin to have a look at one the classic texts of the second century. Over the next six days we'll have read the whole essay in a brief form here, though I would highly recommend making the time to read the full work itself alongside this, as there is so much to glean from it.

The first of his major works (that we still have), this defence of the Faith is addressed to the Roman Emperor with a very long name, Caesar Titus Ælius Adrianus Antoninus Augustus Pius, and his adopted sons and the Senate.

Justin appeals to their sense of justice, love of reason, philosophy and pursuit of truth in order that the charges often brought against Christians may be fully investigated to see whether any punishment should fall upon the Christian population or not.

During this time, Christians were being punished purely for identifying as "Christians" with little more evidence used against them than maybe "evil rumours" which were doing the rounds.

Justin argues that even with convicted criminals, they at least investigate the claims before punishing that person, but in the case of Christians, they only "receive the name as proof" against them, which is unjust.

The Emperor's sons were philosophers, which in Greek and Roman times was more like a profession, which it had its own clothing style to display this (similar to how you'd recognise a vicar/priest today by the white 'dog collar' or robes they wear). To this end, Justin argues that there are those who wear the "garb" of philosophers, but who "do nothing worthy of their profession", yet not all philosophers are punished for this just because they claim the name.

Similarly, there were poets who would get a laugh by insulting the gods and who also "taught atheism", yet to the contrary of how Christians were treated, the Romans "bestow prizes and honours upon those who euphoniously insult the gods"!

"Why, then, should this be?", Justin asks, especially since the Christians "pledge [themselves] to do no wickedness" but yet are still charged with atheism for teaching that the gods of old were in fact demons deceiving the people, calling themselves by different names to be worshipped. Apparently Socrates was killed by men driven with evil passion from demons for trying "to bring these things to light, and deliver men from the demons" and charged "as an atheist and a profane person"[55] — a charge which was similar to that which the Christians were accused of.

Here Justin does a nice contrast between the reasoning used by the Greeks in condemning Socrates, and the pure Reason (Jesus) which condemns them all

---

55 Socrates was also accused of "corrupting the youth" and of impiety. He was executed for this in 399 BC. *cf.* Nails, Debra, "Socrates", *The Stanford Encyclopedia of Philosophy* (Summer 2017 Edition), Edward N. Zalta (ed.), <https://plato.stanford.edu/archives/sum2017/entries/socrates/>

for following demons. The word play is lost in English, but the word for "reason" is *logos* and so he says that the Greeks used their own reasoning (*logos*) to pass judgement, but that they, along with the Barbarians,[56] were condemned by Reason Himself (*the* Logos), "who took shape, and became man, and was called Jesus Christ". It is because of this, Justin argues, that the Christians denounce the gods as being "wicked and impious demons".

Now, to modern ears, what the Christians were accused of will sound strange: their charge was that of *atheism!* But back in the early second century "atheism" was a phrase which was applied to those who denied the Roman gods. Justin gladly admits this too, but with some added clarification; "we confess that we are atheists, so far as gods of this sort are concerned, but not with respect to the most true God, the Father of righteousness".

Justin makes the point that if the Emperor is to try people for wrongdoing, that "each one who is convicted may be punished as an evil-doer, and not as a Christian" — to judge them as a person by their life and deeds, rather than an assumption of them due to a name they claim.

The end part of these opening chapters close off with a denouncement of idols and their futility, since

---

56 Originally, they were people from central and northern Europe, mainly Germanic. In ancient Greece, "barbarian" simply meant someone who didn't speak Greek, and in Roman times it had come to mean any and all foreigners.

they are mere items crafted by men who are "intemperate" and who "are practised in every vice", which is contrasted with the formless God who formed all things and who needs nothing offered to Him, since "He is the provider of all things".

In speaking of how the True God should be worshipped, in contrast with the demonic practices of the Roman gods, Justin explains that;

> [God] accepts those only who imitate the excellences which reside in Him, temperance, and justice, and philanthropy, and as many virtues as are peculiar to a God who is called by no proper name…

Contrasted with "the wicked demons" who work with the "lust of wickedness which is in every man" to draw them to "all manner of vice", the Christian God is a stark contrast to those which the Emperor is familiar, even with regards to the Kingdom which he has heard Christians look for. "You suppose, without making any inquiry, that we speak of a human kingdom", he says, but goes on to explain that it is not so with Christians, since their minds are fixed elsewhere.[57]

This ends the first eleven chapters of this massive and notable apologetic work — part one of six for these daily readings. I hope you enjoy reading this great, classic literary work.

---

57 *cf.* Phil 3:20

Notes

DAY 13

JUSTIN MARTYR:
FIRST APOLOGY, CHAPS. 12-23

From here on, each chapter or so in this apology deals with a different area of Christian doctrine, with succinct arguments for the reality of what is believed and accepted. Because this text is so large, I'm going to try and summarise as much as I can and pull out any of the main points which stand out most for each argument.

Living Righteously

Chapter twelve kicks off straight into a long dialogue about the righteousness of Christians and how they are the Emperor's "helpers and allies in promoting peace" due to their very nature and lifestyle in following Christ. Everyone is under God's watchful eye, Justin argues, no one can "escape the notice of God", and because of this, "each man goes to everlasting punishment or salvation according to the value of his actions".

The point he's trying to make is that if everyone understood this, they should be more inclined to live a virtuous life before God, and that is what the Christians preach. They are not wrongdoers, but rather are trying to counter that behaviour, and if the Emperor honestly valued the truth and wanted to uphold his reputation for "piety and philosophy" he would act reasonably, unless of course he, "like the foolish, prefer custom to truth". Justin didn't mince his words at all, even when speaking to the Emperor!

A Rational Faith

Continuing with the argument for acting rationally towards Christians, Justin outlines how the faith in which they profess, is in actuality, a rational faith.

Before giving an explanation for this, he outlines the history of Christ; that he was born for a purpose and was crucified under Pontius Pilate, and how they learned he was the Son of God to be worshipped.

> …we reasonably worship Him, having learned that He is the Son of the true God Himself, and holding Him in the second place, and the prophetic Spirit in the third, we will prove. For they proclaim our madness to consist in this, that we give to a crucified man a place second to the unchangeable and eternal God, the Creator of all…[58]

Demonic Influences

This is the start of misunderstanding, and Justin goes on to explain how it is the demons he previously mentioned (in the previous chapter) that go about misrepresenting the Christian faith, but in reality, Christians are changed people and the evil and wicked things they once did and loved, they now do the opposite of:

> …we who formerly delighted in fornication, but now

---

58 This is also one of the earliest references to the doctrine of the Trinity.

embrace chastity alone … we who valued above all things the acquisition of wealth and possessions, now bring what we have into a common stock…[59]

But in case it would seem that he is "reasoning sophistically", Justin wants to present quotes from Christ's teaching to prove that "He was no sophist, but His word was the power of God"!

For clarity, since words have changed meaning over time or fallen into disuse, being a "sophist" and speaking "sophistically" was a form of teaching in Greek philosophy. It was a way of reasoning with clever but false or fallacious arguments that just sounded good — whether or not they were accurate or moral was besides the point!

The Teachings Of Jesus

Justin lists out a whole page full of quotes from Jesus, all of which we'd recognise from the Gospels, from his teachings on looking at a women with lust, to divorce, to praying for your enemies to not worrying about life. It's a nice summary of Jesus' moral teachings on the way in which we should strive to live, which Justin then follows on from with more of Jesus' teaching on responding to violence and in swearing oaths saying, "[Jesus] has exhorted us to lead all men, by patience and gentleness, from shame and the love of evil" by which it is proved because many men who were like the Emperor "have changed their violent and tyrannical

59 *cf.* Acts 2:44,45; 4:32

disposition" because of the examples of Christians.

After all of this, Justin then seeks to clarify the difference between those who are Christians in name only, to those who really are followers of Jesus by quoting Matthew 7:21-23 (*Not everyone who says to me, 'Lord, Lord'...*) and saying, "let those who are not found living as He taught, be understood to be no Christians" and in an unexpected turn, he rounds off this section by essentially giving the Emperor permission, or rather, *demanding* it of the Emperor, to punish those who "are not living pursuant to these His teachings, and are Christians only in name"!

Civil Obedience

Quoting more from Jesus, Justin makes the point that "everywhere we, more readily than all men, endeavour to pay to those appointed by you the taxes both ordinary and extraordinary, as we have been taught by [Jesus]". Quoting from Matthew 22:19-21 (*Give therefore to the emperor the things that are the emperor's...*) to back up the point, he goes on to say that as well, Jesus taught them to pray for their rulers, which they do, but that if those rulers "pay no regard to our prayers and frank explanations", then it's no loss to the Christians since they are convinced that the wicked will suffer eternal consequences.

The Resurrection

This one is interesting as Justin contrasts the spiritual

powers that the Emperor will be familiar with from his own divinations, oracles, magi and "Dream-senders and Assistant-spirits (Familiars)" to prove the point that "even after death souls are in a state of sensation" and thus there is an afterlife worth considering. He goes on to say that because these practitioners of divinations etc. are granted favours, that the Christians should also be granted the same because they "more firmly" believe in God, "since we expect to receive again our own bodies" via resurrection.

The resurrection is something which seems to be a sticking point to accept, but they "maintain that with God nothing is impossible" and goes on to contrast the way in which they will be planted like seeds in the ground through death, so that in the future they will come up with new bodies. To try and explain this concept even more, the resurrection is contrasted with "human seed" (i.e. Sperm);

> [If I] were to show you human seed and a picture of a man, and were to say with confidence that from such a substance such a being could be produced, would you believe before you saw the actual production?

Basically, if you'd never known human growth, and someone showed you a drop of fluid and a photo of an adult and said one produced the other, would you believe it if you hadn't already witnessed it to be true? In the same way then, the resurrection happens, and it can only be accepted by those who are willing to believe something which seems impossible, which will, "in God's appointed time rise again and put on incorruption".

Elements Of Truth In Greek Philosophy And Poetry

Justin lists out a few known poets and philosophers of which the Emperor would be familiar with, saying that even these people teach certain aspects which are similar to Christian doctrine; such as, the world was created and arranged by God, as Plato taught; that the souls of the departed are conscious and the wicked ones punished, which the righteous rewarded; which is similar to what he poets and philosophers etc. taught. So now he asks that if "on some points we teach the same things as the poets and philosophers whom you honour", and in some cases go beyond what they say to greater things, "why are we unjustly hated more than all others?".

Further to this argument, Justin then contrasts the history and life of Christ with the Roman gods, such as Jupiter and Mercury, to say that in those accounts the Romans accepts such wonders like virgin births and miraculous healing, so then why should it be so hard to accept that Jesus, though born a man, was in fact the begotten Son of God, the Word (*logos*) made flesh?

Justin closes off his argument to prove that Jesus is superior to these other gods because "what has been taught us by Christ, and by the prophets who preceded Him, are alone true, and are older than all the writers who have existed" which was proven by the Word becoming a man to teach these things "for the conversion and restoration of the human race".

He again mentions about the demonic influences which have had their way through the Greek poets to slander the Christian name and doctrines, to which he will defend next in the following chapters and what we shall read in the next daily reading.

It becomes more and more obvious that there is a spiritual battle going on 'behind the scenes' of life, especially considering these arguments we're just read. Otherwise, if the Greeks were teaching a faith so similar to Christianity in some regards, why would they hate and persecute the Christians so much? The words of Jesus' in Luke 21:17[60] about being hated due to Jesus' name echo very deeply here that's for sure.

---

60 *cf.* Mark 13:13; Matt 10:22

Notes

DAY 14

JUSTIN MARTYR:
FIRST APOLOGY, CHAPS. 24-35

Persecution And False Gods

Mark 13:13

...and you will be hated by all because of my name. But the one who endures to the end will be saved.

This next part of the apology really shows the truth of Jesus' words here. Justin continues on from the thought in his previous chapter (which we saw in yesterday's reading) about how the things which Christians believe are not far off from what the Greek say and believe, yet despite this, they are still "hated on account of the name of Christ". Even though the Greeks worship some animals which others will hunt and eat, and that there is no consensus on which animals are gods and which are food, these people can still worship freely without fear, but Christians are persecuted and threatened with death simply for being called as such.

He then goes on to outline the various different gods and magicians that the Greeks believed in, and how in all of their various and blasphemous ways, yet all under one name or doctrine, they are still free from threat. But even in spite of death, Christians will still worship Jesus because through him they have learned to despise and reject these false gods as demons.

Guilt Of Harming Children

Justin condemns the practices of "exposing children" — which in this context seems to mean sexually abusing them; this could be in relation to the Greek and Roman practice of Pederasty.[61] He explains that Christians have been "taught that to expose newly-born children is the part of wicked men" and to harm any child is to sin against God himself.[62] As the people of old would herd cattle and raise animals for a purpose, so these children "are brought up to prostitution"; like animals they "rear children only for this shameful use".

Justin paints a terrible picture of his contemporary society, in which the people "commit unmentionable iniquities" and in their lust, "may possibly be having intercourse with his own child, or relative, or brother". The level of prostitution sounds like it is in connection with the temples and worship of false gods, which they were selling children and even their own wives into. He mentions that those "whom you esteem gods there is painted a serpent" which Justin uses to lead into his next point that "the prince of the wicked spirits is called the serpent, and Satan, and the devil" bolstering his previous arguments that the "gods" are in fact demons.

Proofs Of Christ's Power And Status From Prophecy

This chapter, and the ones that follow, aim to defend the true power and status of Christ, and dismiss the claim that Jesus performed his "mighty works by magical art, and by this appeared to be the Son of God", and instead was only a mere man empowered by

---

61 Sexual activity involving a man and a boy

62 *cf.* Matt 18:6; Luke 17:2

demons.

To do this, Justin gives a very brief look at the prophets of old who foretold of this coming of the Promised One, healing power, and that he would die and rise again. He was foretold by all the major prophets down through the generations, and was specifically prophesied about coming by Moses, "the first of the prophets". After giving a brief overview of Jesus' birth and how it fulfils the Isaiah prophecy,[63] it is explained, quite strongly, that the virgin conceived a child not through any such lust (as the Greek god Jupiter did), but by the power of God that "overshadowed" Mary got her pregnant.

The explanations given make me think about the time Jesus opened the minds of his disciples to all of the Scriptures and prophecies concerning him:

> **Luke 24:27**
> Then beginning with Moses and all the prophets, he interpreted to them the things about himself in all the scriptures.

Citing more prophecies, Justin goes on to tell how even the place where Jesus would be born was predicted and offers an interesting titbit of historical proof by telling the Emperor that he "can ascertain also from the registers of the taxing made under Cyrenius"[64] that Jesus was, in fact, born in Bethlehem.

---

63 *cf.* Isa. 7:14

64 Also known as *'the Census of Quirinius'*, *cf.* Luke 2:2

Closing his argument and proofs for Jesus being the true Son of God, the incarnate Word (and not simply a man) Justin quotes from Isaiah again, and also the Psalms, to show that even Jesus' death was predicted, down to the nails in his hands and feet.[65]

Interestingly, as further proof to this claim, he tells the Emperor that he can look up the facts of the crucifixion and see "that these things did happen" because he "can ascertain from the Acts of Pontius Pilate" what took place. What's intriguing about this, is that this book which is referenced is known to be of spurious origins, with various later forgeries created to try and discredit Christians even!

If you're interested to see what it says though, you can read a brief scholarly debate in the introduction text of the book online.[66]

In the chapters that follow, Justin continues with the theme of prophecy to further show proofs for Christ being the true manifest Word of God. I pray that you learn and grow in understanding about the things of God from Justin Martyr's arguments, which continue over the following days.

---

65 *cf.* Ps 22:16; Isaiah 58:2; 65:2

66 *cf. Acts of Pilate,* <http://earlychristianwritings.com/actspil-ate.html>

Notes

Notes

DAY 15

JUSTIN MARTYR: FIRST APOLOGY, CHAPS. 36-47

Following on from yesterday's theme of prophecy which predicts Christ, Justin explains the different types, or "modes", of prophetic messages.

From utterances which foretell the future, to speaking on behalf of the Father, he goes on to say how the Jews missed the prophecies that pointed to Jesus — even those which showed that he would be crucified; and so the Jews hate the Christians who keep showing these things from the Scriptures.

What follows is some really interesting interpretation of prophecy in the Old Testament which not only is used to prove the power of God, but also to show that the different ways prophecies are spoken demonstrates who inspired them; i.e. some are from the Father, some Christ and others, the Spirit. This in itself is demonstrating a view of the Trinity within prophecy, too.

The Father

Quoting various passage from Isaiah, Justin makes the point that when a prophecy is spoken from a "thus saith the Lord" perspective, then that is the Father speaking through the prophet; for example —

Isaiah 66:1
Thus says the Lord:
Heaven is my throne
and the earth is my footstool;
what is the house that you would build for me,
and what is my resting place?

The Son

But those times where the prophet speaks a message of suffering, pain or sacrifice from the perspective of God, then it is Christ speaking as the pre-existing Word. He gives various examples from the Psalms and Isaiah to show this, such as:

> **Isaiah 50:6**
> I gave my back to those who struck me,
> and my cheeks to those who pulled out the beard;
> I did not hide my face
> from insult and spitting.

And,

> **Psalms 22:17-18**
> I can count all my bones.
> They stare and gloat over me;
> they divide my clothes among themselves,
> and for my clothing they cast lots.

The Spirit

When it is the the Spirit speaking, it appears to be prophecies which are more in the 3rd person about the Lord and what he will do. Using an example from Isaiah again, Justin gives an example of a prophecy and also goes on to explain how it has been fulfilled through Christ in the Christians who follow him:

Isaiah 2:3-4
For out of Zion shall go forth instruction,
and the word of the Lord from Jerusalem.
He shall judge between the nations,
and shall arbitrate for many peoples;
they shall beat their swords into plowshares,
and their spears into pruning hooks;
nation shall not lift up sword against nation,
neither shall they learn war any more.

I know many people today read this passage as something future and yet to be fulfilled, thinking it is speaking of a global event where *all people* suddenly stop making war. But Justin gives us an example of how early Christians interpreted this, and it's one I've never heard any modern preacher say or teach:

And that it (Isa. 2:3-4) did so come to pass, we can convince you. For from Jerusalem there went out into the world, men, twelve in number, and these illiterate, of no ability in speaking: but by the power of God they proclaimed to every race of men that they were sent by Christ to teach to all the word of God; and we who formerly used to murder one another do not only now refrain from making war upon our enemies, but also, that we may not lie nor deceive our examiners ...

Christ's Appearance And Death Foretold

Continuing with the theme of the prophetic messages, Justin goes to show more examples from the Old

122

Testament which foretold the life of Jesus and "the conspiracy which was formed against Christ by Herod the king of the Jews, and the Jews themselves" because he "thought it right and relevant to mention some other prophetic utterances of David" and goes on to quote the whole of Psalm 2 as his proof.

> Yet have I been set by Him a King on Zion His holy hill, declaring the decree of the Lord. The Lord said to Me, Thou art My Son; this day have I begotten Thee.

And to the death and resurrection of Jesus, he goes on to show that "through the same David, intimated that Christ, after He had been crucified, should reign" and quotes 1 Chron. 16: 23-27 and merges that with Ps. 96 to make up one long prophetic statement, as is the habit of Justin throughout his writings.

There's an interesting bit here where Justin quotes Ps 96:10 as saying: *"Let them rejoice among the nations. The Lord hath reigned from the tree."*

He uses this as his proof for Jesus reigning after his death. But if you look this up in a Bible now, it will say this (differing slightly per translation):

> Say among the nations, "The Lord is king!
> The world is firmly established; it shall never be moved. He will judge the peoples with equity."

Looking a little more into this, it appears that this

quote in *First Apology* is the only ancient Greek text to have this wording. Any other quote of Ps. 96:10 from Tertullian onward (~200 AD), comes purely from the translation in *The Old Latin Version*[67] of the Psalm, which is the Latin Bible that predated the Vulgate Bible.[68]

Prophecy And Free Will

The rest of the chapters go through more examples of prophetic messages and the different types that can be found in the Old Testament, such as explaining that sometimes the Spirit spoke prophecies in the past tense as though they had already happened. To avoid this being used as a reason to misrepresent the message, Justin goes on to explain that the "things which [God] absolutely knows will take place, He predicts as if already they had taken place".

There seemed to be some who would accuse the Christians of believing in fate, and so Justin offers an argument against such thoughts to provide some kind of "prophetic responsibility".

All of our actions, whether good or bad, whether there be rewards or chastisements; all of these are given due to man's own actions. "Since if it be not so, but all things happen by fate, neither is anything at all

---

67 Also known as the *Vetus Latina* Bible. It was widely used by Christian communities from the second century onwards.

68 Pope Damasus I commissioned Jerome to work on the Vulgate in 382 AD as a revision to the Old Latin Bible (*Vestus Latina*).

in our own power", which begins the argument for freedom of will, asserting that if people are fated to do either good or bad, then the one is no more deserving of reward than the other is of punishment.

> And again, unless the human race have the power of avoiding evil and choosing good by free choice, they are not accountable for their actions

He goes on to make the argument that if fate decides how people act, then it is fate which is the cause of evil, and not people, and this is not how God has made mankind to be. To borrow from the terminology of "fate", Justin makes one final point that there is one thing in which the Christians "assert is inevitable fate" — that those who choose good, will be rewarded, and those who choose evil will be punished. By this, prophecy is not nullified by free will, and free will is not overcome by prophecy, but that all which God spoke through his prophets concerning rewards or punishments for the actions of the human race, are still a valid foretelling even with freedom of will, because "God spoke thus to the man first created: 'Behold, before thy face are good and evil: choose the good.'" The choice is there and the foretelling is that of the outcome of our choices.

A couple more topics are covered briefly, such as those who lived before Christ and how salvation affects them (basically it does, because Jesus was the pre-existing Word), and Christ ruling from heaven and the prediction of Judea being made desolate, fulfilling

Isa. 64:10 *("Your holy cities have become a wilderness...).*

Though this has been a long chapter, and not as brief as I would have liked to keep it, there was a lot of topics covered that I thought that it would be an injustice to skip on these things since they are central to some of our understanding of Christ and his relation to being the prophetic fulfilment of the Scriptures.

I recommend that you read the original text of today's chapters to really get an understanding of what Justin was saying and attempting to draw out in order to clarify Christian doctrine properly.

Notes

DAY 16

JUSTIN MARTYR: FIRST APOLOGY, CHAPS. 48-59

In these chapters today, Justin is continuing with his long exposition of the prophecies concerning Christ, covering every aspect of the life, ministry and death of Jesus. He quotes Scripture at length to fully prove his points in order to show the Emperor, to whom he writes, and indeed any of us reading his works today, the undeniable reality that Jesus was the expected and long-awaited Messiah.

I won't quote massive amounts of these chapters, since it would be redundant, so I'll just highlight each prophecy and give the Scriptural references which are used in *First Apology* as proofs for Jesus' Messiahship.

Finding the actual Scriptural quotes to reference is sometimes difficult because Justin has a habit of combining various verses from different chapters of the same prophet into one sentence!

The following Scripture quotes are taken from *First Apology* and are as Justin wrote them.

Christ's Life And Death Foretold

Jesus' life and ministry foretold from a combination of Isa 35:5-6, Isa 32:4 and Isa 26:19 –

> At His coming the lame shall leap as an hart, and the tongue of the stammerer shall be clear speaking: the blind shall see, and the lepers shall be cleansed; and the dead shall rise, and walk about.

And his death from Isaiah 57:1 –

> Behold now the righteous perisheth, and no man layeth
> it to heart; and just men are taken away, and no man
> considereth. From the presence of wickedness is the
> righteous man taken, and his burial shall be in peace:
> he is taken from our midst.

His Rejection By The Jews Foretold

From Isaiah 65:1-3

And the words are spoken as from the person of Christ;
and they are these *"I was manifest to them that asked
not for Me; I was found of them that sought Me not: I
said, Behold Me, to a nation that called not on My
name. I spread out My hands to a disobedient and
gainsaying people, to those who walked in a way that
is not good, but follow after their own sins; a people
that provoketh Me to anger to My face."* For the Jews
having the prophecies, and being always in expectation
of the Christ to come, did not recognise Him; and not
only so, but even treated Him shamefully.

His Humiliation Predicted

From Isaiah 52:13-15, Isaiah 53:1-8

Because they delivered His soul unto death, and He
was numbered with the transgressors, He has borne the
sin of many, and shall make intercession for the
transgressors. For, behold, My Servant shall deal
prudently, and shall be exalted, and shall be greatly
extolled. As many were astonished at Thee, so marred
shall Thy form be before men, and so hidden from
them Thy glory; so shall many nations wonder, and the

kings shall shut their mouths at Him. For they to whom it was not told concerning Him, and they who have not heard, shall understand. O Lord, who hath believed our report? and to whom is the arm of the Lord revealed? We have declared before Him as a child, as a root in a dry ground. He had no form, nor glory; and we saw Him, and there was no form nor comeliness: but His form was dishonoured and marred more than the sons of men. A man under the stroke, and knowing how to bear infirmity, because His face was turned away: He was despised, and of no reputation. It is He who bears our sins, and is afflicted for us; yet we did esteem Him smitten, stricken, and afflicted. But He was wounded for our transgressions, He was bruised for our iniquities, the chastisement of peace was upon Him, by His stripes we are healed. All we, like sheep, have gone astray; every man has wandered in his own way. And He delivered Him for our sins; and He opened not His mouth for all His affliction. He was brought as a sheep to the slaughter, and as a lamb before his shearer is dumb, so He openeth not His mouth. In His humiliation, His judgement was taken away.

The Majesty Of Christ

From Isaiah 53:8-12

His generation who shall declare? Because His life is cut off from the earth: for their transgressions He comes to death. And I will give the wicked for His burial, and the rich for His death; because He did no violence, neither was any deceit in His mouth. And the Lord is pleased to cleanse Him from the stripe. If He be given for sin, your soul shall see His seed prolonged in days. And the Lord is pleased to deliver His soul from grief, to show Him light, and to form Him with knowledge, to justify the righteous who richly serves many. And He shall bear our iniquities. Therefore He shall inherit many, and He shall divide the spoil of the strong; because His soul was delivered to death: and He was numbered with the transgressors; and He bore the sins of many, and He was delivered up for their transgressions.

The Ascension Of Christ

Psalm 24:7-10
Lift up the gates of heaven; be opened, that the King of glory may come in. Who is this King of glory? The Lord, strong and mighty.

From this point on, Justin argues that since he has proven that the prophecies of old have come to pass, then it follows that those which "are yet to come to pass, shall certainly happen".

The General Resurrection And Punishments

Ezekiel 37:7-8; Isaiah 45:24
Joint shall be joined to joint, and bone to bone, and flesh shall grow again; and every knee shall bow to the Lord, and every tongue shall confess Him.

Isaiah 66:24
Their worm shall not rest, and their fire shall not be quenched

The closing chapters of this section deal mostly with an argument against the Roman god Jupiter and how that even though it is related to the people that some are called "sons of Jupiter" by the poets, this is done without any such proof as has been presented about Jesus, yet people believe.

"For with what reason should we believe of a crucified man", Justin argues, "unless we had found testimonies concerning Him published before He came and was born as man" and had seen those things fulfilled.

Justin makes the point again that these other gods were inspired by demons, though not simply by random, but by using the ancient prophecies about Christ as a source to include a seed of truth within. This was done in order to deceive, though the demons, misunderstanding the symbolism of the cross, never made any of their false gods die from crucifixion. Also, people like Plato who alluded to a divine entity being placed "crosswise" at the centre of the universe[69] didn't understand it either, and was in fact borrowing from Moses who wrote these things long before any of the Greek or Roman gods and prophets came along.

There is a lot of doctrine and theology contained in these chapters, much of which is still very relevant for apologetics today, some of it which could even serve as a good starting point in evangelistic outreach.

---

69 *cf. Timaeus,* 34ab and 36bc <http://classics.mit.edu/Plato/timaeus.html>

Even if you're not that interested in apologetics, or evangelising necessarily, I'd recommend everyone take some time to read these, and the preceding, chapters carefully as the prophetic statements about Jesus and their fulfilment in him are the basis and foundation of our faith, and having a solid understanding of this is beneficial for all Christians in all times.

Notes

Notes

DAY 17

JUSTIN MARTYR: FIRST APOLOGY, CHAPS. 60–68

So we come to the final chapters of Justin Martyr's first apology, and what an interesting and lengthy read it has been!

These final chapters move on from prophecies about Christ, and cover a few other areas of Christian doctrine and belief, such as: baptism, the Eucharist and weekly worship among other things.

Plato And The Trinity

The first chapter of this reading today concludes from the previous few about the prophetic announcement of Jesus and how even "heathens" recognise the things God has put in place, even without realising it. Case in point here, Plato.

As touched on in the previous chapter, Plato mentions in his work, *Timaeus of Plato*,[70] about "the Son of God" being placed "crosswise" in the universe, which Justin goes on to say that although Plato misunderstood the symbolism of the cross from the writings of Moses, which he "borrowed in like manner", he inadvertently recognises the Trinity.

Plato does this by saying that the "power next to the first God" which was placed crosswise is second, and then speaks of a third, the Spirit of God, because he read that he "moved over the waters" from Moses.[71]

---

70 *cf. Timaeus,* 34ab and 36bc <http://classics.mit.edu/Plato/tim-aeus.html>

71 *cf.* Gen 1:2

But despite this, Justin closes his argument by reiterating his previous point that because Moses predates all the Greek thinkers and writers, what Christians preach, no matter how similar sounding it is to certain Greek fables and myths, is imitation;

> It is not, then, that we hold the same opinions as others, but that all speak in imitation of ours.

Baptism

There's a short overview of the rite of baptism, and how the message Jesus preached about being born again in John 3:5, was also prophesied by Isaiah:

Isaiah 1:16-20
Wash you, make you clean; put away the evil of your doings from your souls; learn to do well; judge the fatherless, and plead for the widow: and come and let us reason together, says the Lord. And though your sins be as scarlet, I will make them white like wool; and though they be as crimson, I will make them white as snow. But if you refuse and rebel, the sword shall devour you: for the mouth of the Lord has spoken it.

From this, Justin says that those who get baptised "are regenerated in the same manner in which we were ourselves regenerated" and that they "may obtain in the water the remission of sins formerly committed". Justin points out that this is something they have "learned from the apostles", a teaching which bears a striking resemblance to what the apostle Peter writes in 1 Peter 3:21 —

> And baptism, which this prefigured, now saves you — not as a removal of dirt from the body, but as an appeal to God for a good conscience, through the resurrection of Jesus Christ

Baptismal regeneration is something many Evangelical and some Protestant churches would teach against today,[72] as well as find ways to re-interpret 1 Peter, so I find this section particularly interesting as an early perspective and teaching of the Church.[73]

Imitation By demons

Following on with baptism, Justin goes on to say that due to Isaiah prophesying about it, the demons knew what to imitate in the temples of false gods: they would have all their worshippers sprinkled with water on entering and fully immersed on the way out, and also have them remove their shoes as Moses did at the burning bush when "Christ conversed with him under the appearance of fire". This too shows an early example of how Christians viewed the "nameless God [who] spoke to Moses" in light of the revelation of Christ, the Logos.

---

72 Roman Catholicism and Eastern Orthodoxy have some doctrines on salvation and baptism being connected, as do Anglicans and Lutherans to various degrees.

73 Not all Church Fathers affirmed this theological position, at least not outright, so it's not a clear-cut issue.

How God Appeared To Moses

A Christophany is a theological term which typically refers to an appearance or non-physical manifestation of the pre-incarnate Christ in the Old Testament in places where it says that God appeared in some sort of physical or visible form. In a New Testament sense, it could refer to the appearance of a post-ascension Jesus, such as with Paul on Damascus road.

Encouraging anyone who wants to know more about this, Justin says that reading the writings of Moses is the place to go:

> But so much is written for the sake of proving that Jesus the Christ is the Son of God and His Apostle, being of old the Word, and appearing sometimes in the form of fire, and sometimes in the likeness of angels; but now, by the will of God, having become man for the human race.

The Eucharist

This chapter gives us a glimpse at how the early church took Communion together and what it meant for them. For a start, only baptised believers were allowed to partake. Prayers of "considerable length" were then first offered to bless the bread and wine, which upon conclusion, everyone would "salute one another with a kiss"[74] before the "bread and a cup of wine mixed with water" was handed out by the deacons to everyone present. If some were absent that

74 *cf.* Romans 16:16; 1 Cor 16:20; 2 Cor 13:12; 1 Thess. 5:26

day, a portion was kept aside and hand-delivered to those who were away!

It would seem that Justin is teaching either an early form of transubstantiation,[75] or the doctrine of the Real Presence[76] here, similar to what we saw with Ignatius, in that he compares the Word becoming "flesh and blood for our salvation" as the reason why the bread and wine "is the flesh and blood of that Jesus who was made flesh". He also points out that the eating and drinking bread and water, along with some type of ritual, was something which the Mithras cult[77] — those "wicked devils" as Justin calls them — had copied from the Christians and were imitating in their temples.

Weekly Worship

A description follows about how Christians met together to pray and worship on a weekly basis, every Sunday. It's nice to see that some things haven't changed much in over two millennia!

The reason for it being on a Sunday and not the Sabbath is because of the prevailing belief that the world was brought into being on Sunday in the very beginning, and then also the world was again changed on a Sunday when "Jesus Christ our Saviour on the

---

75 The Roman Catholic doctrine that the bread and wine actually become the literal body and blood of Christ

76 The doctrine that Jesus is really or substantially present in the Eucharist, and not only symbolically or metaphorically

77 A pagan religion that worshipped the Sun-god Mithra, which was formed *after* Christianity.

same day rose from the dead".

This is how "church" looked back in Justin Martyr's time:

> And on the day called Sunday, all who live in cities or in the country gather together to one place, and the memoirs of the apostles or the writings of the prophets are read, as long as time permits; then, when the reader has ceased, the president verbally instructs, and exhorts to the imitation of these good things. Then we all rise together and pray, and, as we before said, when our prayer is ended, bread and wine and water are brought, and the president in like manner offers prayers and thanksgivings, according to his ability, and the people assent, saying Amen … And they who are well to do, and willing, give what each thinks fit; and what is collected is deposited with the president, who succours the orphans and widows and those who, through sickness or any other cause, are in want, and those who are in bonds and the strangers sojourning among us, and in a word takes care of all who are in need.

Conclusion

Justin concludes *First Apology* to the Emperor by pleading that, "if these things seem to you to be reasonable and true, honour them; but if they seem nonsensical, despise them as nonsense, and do not decree death against those who have done no wrong" and again urges him to act justly or risk facing the judgement of God.

That's all from Justin Martyr; it's been a very lengthy but informative read that's for sure, offering some very interesting insights into the lives and beliefs of the early Christians. If you haven't read *First Apology* in full, it's something I would recommend that you take the time to do since we've only really scratched the surface here in this book.

Notes

DAY 18

CYPRIAN:
ON THE UNITY OF THE CHURCH,
CHAPS. 1–9

Who: Third century bishop of Carthage (in modern Tunisia), and martyr from Africa

What: A letter to encourage the unity of the church against schisms and heresy during massive Roman persecution.

Why: A disturbance had happened in the church because of a priest called Novatian — a schismatic of the third century, and founder of the sect of the Novatians. Cyprian wrote to counter this and argues that there can only be one united Church, and the Novatian breakaway was in fact a false church. He also argues that Novatian himself was also an antipope.[78]

When: Around 249 - 251 AD

---

78 A false claimant of the Holy See in opposition to a pontiff who was officially elected.

This letter by Cyprian, bishop of Carthage, is apparently one of his greatest works. Written during a time when the new Roman Emperor Decius wanted to restore Rome to its former glory, he decreed that all Christian bishops be killed and any laity to be forced to recant in the face of death.

Many Christians at this time were martyred, but there were also many who also abandoned their faith and sacrificed to the gods in exchange for their lives, or they bought a certificate to say they had sacrificed when they hadn't.[79] This was all considered sin and blasphemy by the Church, though many felt regret and wanted to be forgiven and restored afterwards.

"But how can a man say that he believes in Christ, who does not do what Christ commanded him to do?" Cyprian argues, since the faith of many had become weak.

It is not "persecution alone that is to be feared", Cyprian writes, since "caution is more easy where danger is manifest" but to be all the more vigilant in times of peace because the enemy "creeps on us secretly" in sneaky ways, which is why he has earned

---

79 This is a period of time known as the *Decian persecution,* although it's not clear whether it was targetting Christians specifically. Around 249-250 AD, Emperor Decius issued an edict requiring everyone in the Roman Empire to sacrifice to the Roman gods and in return you would receive a certificate to prove you had done so. Refusal to sacrifice resulted in arrest and death. Christians who refused received the title of "confessors", whilst those who complied with the edict were termed "lapsed" by the Church.

the name "Serpent".

It's in the midst of all of this that a priest called Novatian rose up as an "antipope" (someone who rejected the people's choice of pope and opposed Rome) and caused a schism saying he wanted to restore the "true Church" and drew some people away. Cyprian is arguing for unity and that there is only one true Church and that is those who are all in unity with one another in the local congregation, and also with their Bishops, who by extension should be united in doctrine across all the churches, thus creating the unified Body of Christ. So with that in mind, much of what he writes here is speaking about how the true followers of Christ should act and what they should be doing if they are working out their salvation.

He writes that they (and us today, even) should avoid slipping back into the ways of the "old man" (our pre-conversion mindset and lifestyle), and instead stand strong "in the footsteps of a conquering Christ" so that we can avoid the nets of death and instead "possess the immortality that we have received". Which we do by keeping the commandments of Jesus, "whereby death is driven out and overcome",[80] and go from slaves to sin to friends of God.[81]

What could me more "crafty", he goes on to say, than someone, inspired by the enemy, who invents "heresies and schisms" under the very name of

---

80 *cf.* Matthew 19:17

81 *cf.* John 15:14

"Christian" to deceive those who are weak in their faith. This is why the Church needs to be aware of the enemy and to really persevere in their faith and in keeping the commandments of Christ lest "he might subvert the faith, might corrupt the truth, might divide the unity" and snatch "men from the Church itself"!

These people whom the enemy deceives, "do not stand firm with the Gospel of Christ, and with the observation and law of Christ, they still call themselves Christians, and, walking in darkness, they think that they have the light". Cyprian has strong words and feelings about this matter, lives are at stake, and this schism is potentially leading many astray.

> ...while the adversary is flattering and deceiving, who, according to the apostle's word, transforms himself into an angel of light, and equips his ministers as if they were the ministers of righteousness, who maintain night instead of day, death for salvation, despair under the offer of hope, perfidy under the pretext of faith, antichrist under the name of Christ... [82]

Deception can easily creep in "so long as we do not return to the source of truth, as we do not seek the head nor keep the teaching of the heavenly Master".

"Does he who does not hold this unity of the Church think that he holds the faith?" Cyprian asks, really hammering home the point of keeping unity within the Church and the faith; as Christ endowed the

---

82 *cf.* 2 Corinthians 11:13-15; 1 Jn 2:22; 4:3

Twelve with power, but commissioned Peter to feed the sheep, in doing so Jesus arranged the "origin of that unity" for which the partnership of the Apostles began the Church. To strengthen his argument for unity within One Church, he quotes Paul in Ephesians 4:4-6 (*There is one body and one Spirit...*), calling it the "sacrament of unity" by which we know the true Church.

In speaking of the Bishops, or the "episcopate", Cyprian says they above all need to uphold this unity of faith, because they are "held by each one for the whole" so that they are undivided as the Church is undivided and one.[83]

I like the analogy Cyprian uses to describe the unity and "oneness" of the Church, in comparing it to things in nature:

> As there are many rays of the sun, but one light; and many branches of a tree, but one strength based in its tenacious root; and since from one spring flow many streams, although the multiplicity seems diffused in the liberality of an overflowing abundance, yet the unity is still preserved in the source.

---

83 As an aside, for those interested in Textual Criticism, this paragraph references chapter five of the epistle, which, along with chapter four also, comes from a dual textual traditional. Chapters four and five exist in differing forms in the *Primacy Text* (PT) and in the *Textus Receptus* (TR), which you can read more about in depth in *Popular Patristics volume 32*, Introduction, Section 5.3 "The Textual Tradition", pp. 42-44 by Allen Brent. This book uses a source which is based on the TR tradition.

Separate a ray of the sun from its body of light, its unity does not allow a division of light; break a branch from a tree,--when broken, it will not be able to bud; cut off the stream from its fountain, and that which is cut off dries up. Thus also the Church, shone over with the light of the Lord, sheds forth her rays over the whole world, yet it is one light which is everywhere diffused, nor is the unity of the body separated.

To further show the Church should be in perfect unity, Cyprian quotes Jesus saying "The Father and I are one",[84] and also makes what is a potentially early witness to the disputed *Comma Johanneum*[85] (1 John 5:7-8), when he writes, "again it is written of the Father, and of the Son, and of the Holy Spirit, 'And these three are one'".

Using these verses, he argues that if this unity is "divine strength and coheres in celestial sacraments" can the Church then be separated by opposition?

He who does not hold this unity does not hold God's law, does not hold the faith of the Father and the Son, does not hold life and salvation.

Who, then, is so wicked and faithless, who is so insane

---

84 *cf.* John 10:30

85 The *Johannine Comma*, is a section of additional words in 1 John 5:7-8 which appear in some early Greek texts (eg. *Erasmus*), and also appear in the Latin Vulgate, as well as the King James Version of the Bible. Most modern translations footnote this section.

with the madness of discord, that either he should believe that the unity of God can be divided, or should dare to rend it – the garment of the Lord – the Church of Christ?

This argument about the garment comes from the robe which Jesus wore at his crucifixion which the soldiers cast lots for since they didn't want to rip it. The robe was made of a seamless thread from top to bottom, just as Christ is the head of the Church woven down from heaven to the Body, it too cannot be broken by those who possess it, as it shows the "coherent concord of our people who put on Christ".[86]

To close this section, the argument for unity rests in those words of Jesus previously quoted and also in what Paul wrote when he urged the Corinthians to keep in unity and avoid schisms:

1 Corinthians 1:10
Now I appeal to you, brothers and sisters, by the name of our Lord Jesus Christ, that all of you be in agreement and that there be no divisions among you, but that you be united in the same mind and the same purpose.

As the "Holy Spirit came as a dove, a simple and joyous creature ... This is the simplicity that ought to be known in the Church". Cyprian ends this chapter with this thought, and it is something that the Church

---

86 *cf.* Jn 19:24; Rom 13:14; Gal 3:27

today should do well to remember and hold to, so that there may be unity across the world in true brotherly love, as Jesus said in John 13:34-35 —

I give you a new commandment, that you love one another. Just as I have loved you, you also should love one another. By this everyone will know that you are my disciples, if you have love for one another.

Notes

Notes

DAY 19

CYPRIAN:
ON THE UNITY OF THE CHURCH,
CHAPS. 10–18

Continuing on from yesterday's theme about those who depart from the true and unified Church, Cyprian moves into saying that this is the reason heresies are frequently appearing — because "a discordant faithlessness does not maintain unity".

> **1 John 2:19**
> They went forth from us, but they were not of us; for if they had been of us, surely they would have continued with us.

He goes on to say that the "Lord permits and suffers these things to be" so that personal liberty may still exist, but that God will use this disunity for his own glory to show which church/doctrine is genuine in contrast to the false, as Paul wrote to the Corinthians:

> **1 Corinthians 11:19**
> Indeed, there have to be factions (*Gk. Heresies*) among you, for only so will it become clear who among you are genuine.

These schismatics (or heretics) sit "in the seat of pestilence", Cyprian says, referencing Psalm 1. He has much harsher words about them too, which I am going to quote in full below, so that you can really understand just how serious this matter of creating heresy and schism was taken:

> [They are] deceiving with serpent's tongue, and artful in corrupting the truth, vomiting forth deadly poisons from pestilential tongues; whose speech does creep like

a cancer, whose discourse forms a deadly poison in the heart and breast of every one.

No minced words here, that's for sure! These are also the people Jeremiah prophesied about too, he says, quoting Jer. 2:13; 27:15; 23:21-22 as one combined paragraph against the heretics, which can be summarised as: *"...I have not sent them, says the Lord, but they are prophesying falsely in my name..."*.

Explaining more about how these schismatics operate, Cyprian points to Matthew 18:20 — *"For where two or three are gathered in my name, I am there among them"*, and explains that this verse has been abused and misinterpreted by these heretics for their own ends as a way of saying their church gatherings are just as valid as the rest.

He goes on to say that these "false interpreters of the Gospel" only quote the last few words, ignoring the previous verses, and so cut themselves off from the Church just as they cut off the Lord's words from these verses.

Quoting the full statement from Jesus (vv. 19,20), Cyprian goes on to bring quite an in depth interpretation of these verses and explains what they do and don't mean.

Matthew 18:19-20
Again, truly I tell you, if two of you agree on earth about anything you ask, it will be done for you by my Father in heaven. For where two or three are gathered

in my name, I am there among them.

There are a few preachers today, mostly within the *Prosperity Gospel* movement, who would claim this verse means that you can literally ask for anything and have it (and if you don't get it, then it's your own lack of faith stopping you). Cyprian interprets this instruction by Jesus as a way of him urging for "unanimity and peace upon His disciples" in the things which they pray for; that they are all of one mind and purpose when they come together and come before God. This is similar then to what Jesus says in John 17:11 where he prays for his disciples to "be one, as [He and the Father] are one". This means that when two or three are gathered in His name, Jesus is "showing that most is given, not to the multitude, but to the unanimity of those that pray".

When Jesus says "I am with them", it is meaning that he is "with the simple and peaceable — with those who fear God and keep God's commandments" and goes on to give some examples from Scripture based on this, such as; Shadrach, Meshach, and Abednego being in one accord with their prayers in the fiery furnace, and Christ came among them to deliver them; and again in Acts 5:17-20 (or Acts 16:25-26) when the Apostles were arrested and put in prison, but then were miraculously delivered because they, and the Church, were "simple-minded and of one mind" in what they asked for.

This single-minded unity of prayer and purpose is

asked of by Jesus because, *"He is rather with two or three who pray with one mind, than with a great many who differ"* — a powerful statement indeed.

But not only this, to ensure full unity within the Church body, Cyprian then says that when Jesus "gave the law of prayer", he made sure to add a prerequisite, so that everyone who asks of God, may be required to live in unity with one another if they expect to be heard. This is why in Mark 11:25, Jesus says, when "you stand praying, forgive, if you have anything against anyone" because then God "calls back from the altar one who comes to the sacrifice in strife, and bids him first agree with his brother, and then return with peace and offer his gift to God", therefore requiring unity and peace with one another at all times.

Stronger still, Cyprian goes further to say that even if those who have separated from the Church were to be martyred for the name of Jesus, that this wouldn't ensure they were crowned with righteousness and enter the Kingdom, since "he cannot show himself a martyr who has not maintained brotherly love". Using 1 Cor 13 to back up his point, Cyprian goes on to say that though they may die or do works, to do it without love and unity of the Church, it is nothing; to not remain in the unified brotherly love of the Church Body is to also go against what John wrote in his letters about loving one another and being born of God.[87]

"For both to prophesy and to cast out devils, and to do great acts upon the earth is certainly a sublime and

87 *cf.* 1 John 4:7-8;12

an admirable thing" — but these things do not guarantee the Kingdom to you, as Jesus made clear in Matthew 7:21-23 *("...Not everyone who says to me, 'Lord, Lord,'...")*, "unless he walks in the observance of the right and just way" of Christ and the Church, as outlined by Jesus in Mark 12:29-31, which teaches love and unity in one:

> Jesus answered, "The first is, 'Hear, O Israel: the Lord our God, the Lord is one; you shall love the Lord your God with all your heart, and with all your soul, and with all your mind, and with all your strength.' The second is this, 'You shall love your neighbour as yourself.' There is no other commandment greater than these."

But what peace, love and unity can one keep if "with the madness of discord, [he] divides the Church, destroys the faith, disturbs the peace, dissipates charity, [and] profanes the sacrament?". To answer this, Cyprian quotes from 2 Tim 3:1-9 and basically says *"but what did you expect to happen?",* since the Apostle Paul already predicted through the Holy Spirit that these things would come to pass.

Despite this, and the schisms and those who would cause them, Cyprian says that this shouldn't worry the believers "but rather strengthen [their] faith in the truthfulness". Referencing Jesus' words when he says that the "blind lead the blind",[88] he warns that if any come across these people, to avoid them so as not to be

---

88 *cf.* Matthew 15:14

lead astray by blind leaders and thus "fall into the ditch".

Cyprian closes up this chapter with a recap of various times in the past when the people of God rebelled against God's appointed leaders and Laws, and how they faced the consequences for their actions by being judged by God. One such example that Cyprian gives is the rather drastic event in Num 26:9-10 when the earth opened up and swallowed those who rebelled!

I think the point is clear: Jesus is the head of the Church, and those who would try to divide his Body takes a grave risk of provoking the anger of the Lord against them and any who should follow their deception.

Notes

Notes

DAY 20

CYPRIAN:
ON THE UNITY OF THE CHURCH,
CHAPS. 19–27

Here we come to the final chapters of Cyprian's letter. This flows straight on from yesterday's judgement on those who would draw people away from the Church towards their own schisms and heresies. Though, he makes a distinction between those who have lapsed in their faith, and those who intentionally lead people astray;

> ...on the one hand, he who has lapsed has only injured himself; on the other, he who has endeavoured to cause a heresy or a schism has deceived many by drawing them with him. In the former, it is the loss of one soul; in the latter, the risk of many.

He goes on to say that if you go astray through lack of discipline or temptation, then you can repent and be forgiven, but the intentional heretics risk unforgiveness and their souls; hence why it is written, he says, "hold fast to what you have, so that no one may seize your crown".[89]

Speaking more about the crowns we attain, Cyprian delves into confessing sins and how that the mere act of confession doesn't save us or give us the "full desert of the crown", but "it initiates our dignity" which is why Jesus said, "the one who endures to the end will be saved".[90] Everything we do and say during our Christian walk in this life is a "step by which we ascend to the summit of salvation", and not the summit itself, which is why we need to watch ourselves and

89 *cf.* Rev 3:11

90 *cf.* Matt 24:13

keep on the narrow path because every time we repent and confess our sins, "the adversary is more provoked"!

"For the Lord chose Judas also among the apostles", Cyprian points out, even though Judas betrayed the Lord afterwards. This didn't break the faith of the Apostles, and neither should it break us by seeing those in the Church fall away, as sad as it may be. We are a corporate Body together in the Faith, but our salvation is our own to "work out with fear and trembling"[91] and isn't dependant on anyone else, even though they may be someone you respect and find encouraging.

As Paul wrote to the Roman church, saying a similar message, God is not diminished by what we do:

Romans 3:3-4
What if some were unfaithful? Will their faithlessness nullify the faithfulness of God? By no means! Although everyone is a liar, let God be proved true.

But if these leaders who have caused schisms and dissent cannot be brought back with "wholesome council", then those who are ensnared in the deceit need to "loose [themselves] from the nets of deceit, free [their] wandering steps from errors, [and] acknowledge the straight way of the heavenly road". But if they don't, then those Christians who have not been deceived should heed the advice of Paul when he

91 *cf.* Phil. 2:12

says, "withdraw yourself from all brethren who walk disorderly"[92] and to also "let no man deceive you with vain words",[93] for the wrath of God is upon these people. Therefore, flee from them, "lest, while anyone is associated with those who walk wickedly … should be found in like guilt".

And just as Paul also wrote in Eph 4:4-6, Cyprian echoes this sentiment to back his point about keeping in unity with one another:

> God is one, and Christ is one, and His Church is one, and the faith is one, and the people is joined into a substantial unity of body by the cement of concord.

So just like a physical, human body can't be torn into pieces and broken up, neither can the *true* Church body be dis-unified.

Before he went to his passion, Jesus left us with a heritage of peace that he gives to us and leaves with us[94] so that we may be called "sons of God";[95]

> If we are fellow-heirs with Christ, let us abide in the peace of Christ; if we are sons of God, we ought to be peacemakers.[96]

---

92 *cf.* 2 Thess. 3:6

93 *cf.* Eph. 5:6

94 *cf.* John 14:27

95 *cf.* Matt. 5:9

96 *cf.* Rom. 8: 14, 17

Pointing back to the Apostles, Cyprian references the book of Acts, when "the whole group of those who believed were of one heart and soul" and that they "were constantly devoting themselves to prayer[97] … and thus they prayed with effectual prayers; thus they were able with confidence to obtain whatever they asked from the Lord's mercy."

But now he laments because the "unanimity is diminished" among the believers and no longer do they sell their possessions or share things for the common good, as the Church once did. Now, he observes, "we do not even give the tenths from our patrimony (inheritance)" and would rather buy than sell to store up treasures in heaven, "Thus has the vigour of faith dwindled away among us; thus has the strength of believers grown weak.".

Quoting Luke 18:8 about whether Jesus will find faith on earth, Cyprian says that this has now come to pass with the Church becoming idle and lazy in their faith, since many no longer take the teaching of the Gospel seriously. Closing off his letter, Cyprian tries to encourage the Church to muster itself up out of this drowsy, unenthusiastic state, and turn back to the vigour they once had, just as those who came before them also had.

> Let us, beloved brethren, arouse ourselves as much as we can; and breaking the slumber of our ancient listlessness … If these commands be observed, if these warnings and precepts be kept, we cannot be overtaken

---

97 *cf.* Acts 1:14; 4:32

in slumber by the deceit of the devil; but we shall reign with Christ in His kingdom as servants that watch.

This message holds just as much truth for the Church today, even after all this time. Cyprian's words ring true throughout history and serve as a timeless reminder to not forsake our first love and turn back to Jesus with our passion and joy renewed![98]

---

98 *cf.* Rev 2:4-5

Notes

DAY 21

ATHANASIUS: LIFE OF ANTHONY, CHAPS. 1–10

Who: Athanasius, Bishop of Alexandria; Confessor[99] and Doctor of the Church;[100] born c. 296; died 2 May, 373 AD. He was the main defender of orthodoxy in the 4th-century battle against the Arianism heresy.[101] Certain writers received the title "Doctor" on account of the great advantage their doctrine had on the whole Church, Athanasius especially for his doctrine on the incarnation.

What: The biography of *Anthony the Great,* the so-called Father of Monasticism, which helped to spread the concept of Christian monasticism, particularly in Western Europe.

Why: From the letter's own prologue: *"The life and conversation of our holy Father, Anthony: written and sent to the monks in foreign parts by our Father among the Saints, Athanasius, Bishop of Alexandria."* The monks wanted an accurate account of Anthony's life so that they could better imitate his life and teachings.

When: Somewhere between 356 and 362 AD

---

99 A title of honour to designate those brave champions of the Faith who had confessed Christ publicly during persecution and had suffered the consequences for doing so.

100 This was a title given to certain people on account of the great advantage the whole Church has obtained from their doctrine.

101 Arianism: a doctrine about Christ which taught that Jesus was created by God and was not eternal like the Father. It was denounced as a heresy by the Council of Nicaea in 325 AD.

When I first came across this text, I didn't know anything about it, except that I'd heard the name before. After a little background research,[102] I was excited to read this as it was a very influential text — not only for the Church as a whole in setting the way for ascetic monasticism — but on convicting a great many who read it, bringing them to conversion. One such notable person who came to the faith because of Anthony's biography, was Augustine.[103]

Athanasius, knowing the influence of Anthony's life, opens his letter by saying that: "I know that you, when you have heard ... will be wishful to emulate [Anthony's] ... pattern of discipline". Being a bit partial to the monastic lifestyle myself, I was initially curious to see how I personally responded to this biography as well — and I was not disappointed.

In this letter, Athanasius says he planned to enquire of those monks who had spent more time with "Anthony the Great",[104] but due to the season of sailing coming to an end, and the letter being urgent, he decided to instead write down all that he personally knew about Anthony. Athanasius had met Anthony many times before because he "was his attendant for a

---

102 Wright, D. (1999, Oct 01) *The Life Changing "Life of Antony"* Retrieved from http://www.christianitytoday.com/history/issues/issue-64/life-changing-life-of-antony.html

103 *Augustine of Hippo* was an early North African theologian and philosopher (354 – 430).His writings had great influences on Western Christianity and philosophy.

104 He's called "Great", amongst other titles, due to his influence and to also distinguish him from other saints called Anthony.

long time", and so he had learned much from him.

Anthony was of Egyptian descent, from an affluent Christian family, but growing up he didn't rely on his family's wealth. Instead he endeavoured to live a simple life like he saw from Jacob in Genesis;

> **Genesis 25:27**
> When the boys grew up, Esau was a skilful hunter, a man of the field, while Jacob was a quiet man, living in tents.

At around eighteen his parents died leaving him to look after his sister, but it didn't deter him from going to "the Lord's house" as was his custom, upon which "he communed with himself and reflected as he walked how the Apostles left all and followed the Saviour;[105] and how they in the Acts sold their possessions".[106]

Upon entering a church service one day, Matthew 19:21 was being read where Jesus tells the rich man to sell all of his possessions. It struck Anthony as though it had been selected and read out just for him, and so he "went out immediately from the church, and gave the possessions of his forefathers to the villagers", and sold everything else he had and gave the money to the poor, keeping only a little back for his sister.

---

105 *cf.* Matthew 4:20
106 *cf.* Acts 4:34

Early Ascetic Life

Again, at a later time while he was at a church service, he heard a reading from Matthew 6:34 where Jesus teaches us not to worry about the next day because God is in control of our needs. So, like before, he ran out of the church and gave away the last little bit he'd kept aside for himself and his sister. After doing this, he committed his sister to a well respected convent to be raised by nuns, and then he went away from his home to dedicate himself to ascetic discipline (such as prayer, solitude and self control).

There weren't many monasteries in Egypt at this time, so Anthony eventually went into the desert to find greater solitude for prayer and discipline, which was an unusual and unique practice at this time, since other ascetics and monks would just stay in remote places near their villages.

In the next village there was an old man who had been a hermit since his youth. Anthony sought him out to learn piety from and then went about his own discipline, incorporating what he'd learnt. As he heard about other similar men, Anthony would travel far and wide to find them and learn what he could, "having got from the good man as it were supplies for his journey in the way of virtue" before returning home again. Then he "would strive to unite the qualities of each, and was eager to show in himself the virtues of all".

He observed the graciousness of one; the unceasing prayer of another; he took knowledge of another's freedom from anger and another's loving-kindness; he gave heed to one as he watched, to another as he studied; one he admired for his endurance, another for his fasting and sleeping on the ground; the meekness of one and the long-suffering of another he watched with care, while he took note of the piety towards Christ and the mutual love which animated all.

When his reputation had spread throughout the villages, the people "saw that he was a man of this sort, used to call him God-beloved. And some welcomed him as a son, others as a brother".

But as we draw closer to God, the more attention we can also draw from our adversary, the devil. Having seen that someone so young could be so pious, the enemy began "whispering to him the remembrance of his wealth, care for his sister, claims of kindred, love of money [and] love of glory" trying to cloud his mind with the things of the world.

During this time, the devil went to great lengths to tempt and attack Anthony to try and cause him to stumble. In various ways and forms (some physical, even!) the devil took his best shots but Anthony put his mind to Christ and the Scriptures to overcome these trials.

"All this was a source of shame to his foe. For he, deeming himself like God, was now mocked by a young man" — Anthony overcame the devil's attacks and made him look foolish in his attempts. It was because of his faith and trust in Christ's death and resurrection, that those "who truly fight can say, 'not I but the grace of God which was with me'"[107] because we can do nothing of our own.

Not boasting nor being puffed up in this victory, he, "having learned from the Scriptures that the devices of the devil are many,[108] zealously continued the discipline", because he knew that the devil "would endeavour to ensnare him by other means" still.

Continuing more with his ascetic discipline, he would not focus nor remember the past, but would press on with the current day and what lay before, meditating on Paul's words in Philippians 3:14; *"I press on toward the goal for the prize of the heavenly call of God in Christ Jesus."*

Battles With Demons

Eventually, Anthony withdrew to a burial ground far from his village and set up camp in a tomb. He had friends lock him in, but they would return every few of days with bread and water for him.

But the enemy "could not endure it" and thought that within a short time "Anthony would fill the desert with the discipline" and so one night a multitude of demons came to Anthony and physically attacked him, cutting up his back with "stripes". In the morning, his

---

107 *cf.* 1 Corinthians 15:10

108 *cf.* Ephesians 6:11

friends found him and though that he was dead!

Upon waking up, he was taken back to the tomb where the devil once again tried to attack him, but this time with loud noises as though there were an earthquake, and with many terrible apparitions of wild beasts trying to come at him. Though this made Anthony's body ache from the wounds, his mind was clear and he rebuked the demons, unafraid, because "faith in our Lord is a seal and a wall of safety to us".

At this time, he had another vision where it appeared that the roof of the tomb opened up, and rays of light spewed in, causing the demons to vanish and his body to heal and be freed of pain. But pondering on this, he asked of the Lord, "Where were you? Why not do this in the beginning, why wait?" to which the Lord responded in saying that he was always with him, but waited to see how he fought the enemy and whether he endured or was made worse. After this, he was filled with strength, more than he thought he had before, and went on his way. By this point, Anthony was around thirty-five years old.

Anthony's life is obviously very different to most, and this text is much different to the previous epistles we've read so far. The spiritual experiences he has intensifies too, which we'll see as we continue to read on. I hope you look forward to reading more tomorrow to see how Anthony progresses in his new ascetic life, and to vicariously go on the journey with him through Athanasius' telling of Anthony's life story.

Notes

DAY 22

ATHANASIUS:
LIFE OF ANTHONY,
CHAPS. 11-20

Today we will see that what began as a simple desire for personal growth with God, eventually became one of the most influential movements within early Christianity, which affected the faith as a whole, for all time.

Anthony is regarded as the father and founder of desert monasticism, and later on, the group collectively known as the Desert Fathers.[109] Today we will see how it all began.

The old hermit that Anthony had met previously, he asked to go into the desert to dwell with him so that they could be "more eagerly bent on the service of God". But the old man declined due to his age, and also because "there was no such custom" of living in the desert, so Anthony left and went to live on his own in the desert mountains where the devil attacked him again.

Twenty Years Of Solitude

After going into the desert, Anthony arrived at the Nile and found an abandoned fort on the other side of the river where he set up camp to live, surviving only on bread which was brought to him by some friends every so often.

---

109 The Desert Fathers (and also the *Desert Mothers*) were early Christian hermits, nuns and monks who lived in the desert of Egypt around the third century AD. Their collective wisdom and writings still exist today in the book called the *Apophthegmata Patrum* ("Sayings of the Fathers").

Anthony spent *twenty years* alone in this fort, save for the demonic attacks he suffered. At one point the attacks were so intense that the nearby villagers thought he was under physical attack from men, but discovered him alone and in prayer, singing praises and hymns to God.

When two decades has passed, he finally left the fort to find a great crowd had amassed waiting for him so they could learn of his discipline.

On seeing Anthony, though, they were all amazed because his body was "as before", and was neither "fat, like a man without exercise, nor lean from fasting and striving with the demons". In this moment, being full of the Spirit, "through [Anthony] the Lord healed the bodily ailments of many present, and cleansed others from evil spirits" and with godly wisdom he counselled many people in need.

After this, he began preaching from Romans 8:32 about how God didn't hold anything back, but gave up even his only Son, "exhorting all to prefer the love of Christ before all that is in the world", which led many to prefer the solitary life of devotion to God than to their worldly pleasures, and eventually caused many groups to gather in the mountains, and soon "the desert was colonised by monks, who came forth from their own people, and enrolled themselves for the citizenship in the heavens".

To me, that seems pretty amazing — that such conviction could fall on so many people to die to self and truly live a live devoted to God at the expense of the world — it's inspiring I think, and not something you see a great deal of happening today on that kind of level (in the Western Church at least from my experience, and not *en masse* like this).

Monastic Communities Form

As more monks gathered in the desert, they came to Anthony to hear what he could teach them. He gave basic rules, saying that "the Scriptures are enough for instruction, but it is a good thing to encourage one another in the faith, and to stir up with words". He also taught them to take what they learnt and to pass it on to others; and also to keep strong in their devotion to God so that they may gain their inheritance of eternal life when they pass from this life.

> Nor let us think, as we look at the world, that we have renounced anything of much consequence, for the whole earth is very small compared with all the heaven … Therefore let the desire of possession take hold of no one, for what gain is it to acquire these things which we cannot take with us?

He encouraged his followers to not grow weary of their devotion and discipline, but to keep their focus right, similar to what Paul wrote in Colossians 3:2 about setting your mind on things above, and again, in Philippians 3:14, about pressing on towards the goal and heavenly prize of Christ; to "die daily" to self and keep pressing on in Christ, as Paul also wrote in 1 Corinthians 15:31.

"Wherefore having already begun and set out in the way of virtue, let us strive the more that we may attain those things that are before", Anthony taught, not to "feel regret and to be once more worldly-minded", basing his interpretation and teaching on Luke 9:62 *("No one who puts a hand to the plow and looks back is fit for the kingdom of God")*.

Contrasting entering the Kingdom of God with how other nations attain the things they want, Anthony uses the example of the Greeks. They cross seas to gain knowledge, but believers have no need to do that, since Jesus had already said that "the kingdom of heaven is within you" (Luke 17:21), so we "have no need to depart from home for the sake of the kingdom of heaven, nor to cross the sea for the sake of virtue".

His encouragement here, I think, is that no matter where we are, and whatever capacity we have (or don't have), we have no excuse nor reason to not do the work of the Kingdom which Jesus has assigned us all to do in the Great Commission.

This reminds me of my favourite Scripture, which always encourages me and seems fitting to add, so I'll end today's chapter with it, hopefully as encouragement to those reading this:

Acts 20:24
But I do not count my life of any value to myself, if

only I may finish my course and the ministry that I received from the Lord Jesus, to testify to the good news of God's grace.

Amen, may we all press on towards the goal set before us by Christ Jesus.

Notes

DAY 23

ATHANASIUS: LIFE OF ANTHONY, CHAPS. 21–30

Today, we continue with the next part of Athanasius's biography of *'Anthony the Great'*. Anthony had been living in solitude for twenty years in a fort by the Nile, which he recently emerged from. Here he continues his teaching to the people from the surrounding villages.

Beginning with teaching from James,[110] he gives warnings on how we should avoid being led by anger and lust, because they will lead us to death and not into God's righteousness. Instead he instructs that we must be watchful against our desires and the enemy, guarding our hearts,[111] since that can lead us down a path towards deception and sinfulness.

We Battle Against Demonic Forces

From here he begins some lengthy teaching on how our battles aren't against flesh and blood, but the "authorities", "cosmic powers" and the "spiritual forces of evil in the heavenly places",[112] whose number is great in the "air around us", he says.

Going into a little more detail on the deceptions of demons, Anthony explains how that the more Christian's press into God and keep good discipline for living a Christ-like life, the more often demons will throw temptations and evil thoughts our way to try and distract us and cause us to stumble. But with prayer and fasting we can overcome and strengthen our

---

110 *cf.* James 1:14-15,20

111 *cf.* Prov. 4:23

112 *cf.* Eph 6:12

resolve against their attacks, which we'll need since once we defeat the weaker demons by our faith, they will come with stronger powers to try and bring fear through terrible visions and dreams and false prophecies. Through the power of Christ though, these demons are displaced "like serpents and scorpions to be trodden underfoot by us Christians".

Despite this, they will try all the more to distract and deceive the Christian, causing noise and music and sleepless nights by rousing us awake at all hours, sometimes taking on the appearance of holy men or angels in order to trick us into listening to their lies. Even if, Anthony says, they take on the appearance of seemingly godly beings or people, and even if they speak things which have a sliver of truth or quote Scripture (for even Satan quoted Scripture to Jesus in the desert, and the demoniacs declared Jesus to be the Son of God), pay no heed since they do not do this to aid our discipline of righteousness, but rather to tire us out and lead us to abandon the principles of the faith out of despair and from feeling burdened.

> For the demons do all things — they prate, they confuse, they dissemble, they confound — to deceive the simple. They din, laugh madly, and whistle; but if no heed is paid to them forthwith they weep and lament as though vanquished.

Though they may attack us with temptations and evil, ungodly thoughts, like fiery darts flung at our minds, we must remember that "the one who is in you is greater than the one who is in the world".[113] Anthony also makes the point that by "much prayer and of discipline, that when a man has received through the Spirit the gift of discerning spirits, he may have power to recognise their (the demons) characteristics", so that we may be like the Apostles who were "not ignorant of [Satan's] devices".[114]

Whenever I Am Weak, Then I Am Strong

Anthony continues with his teaching on demons and their deceptions, but stresses time and again that though they make much noise, or bring terrible visions, they are powerless and weak — "demons like these, who have no power, try to terrify at least by their displays"; they are like "actors on the stage changing their shape and frightening children with tumultuous apparition and various forms" but, and this is the important point he makes, "now we are gathered together and speak against them, and they know when we advance they grow weak". The more we gather together in prayer and discipline of our faith towards Christ, living a godly and righteous life as the Scriptures instruct, the weaker the enemy becomes and the easier it is for us to ignore him and "his devices".

Casting our minds back to the story of Job, Anthony poses the hypothetical question: "if the devil is so weak, how come Job was overcome with calamity?",

---

113 *cf.* 1 John 4:4
114 *cf.* 2 Cor 2:11

to which he responds by reminding us that despite the devil bringing lots of suffering, illness and sometimes death, to Job or his family and livestock, none of it was possible without permission from God.

"The devil was not the strong man", he points out, because it was God who let Job be tried to test his faith; "certainly he had no power to do anything" other than what was permitted. This, he says, is exactly what proves that the devil is weak because although Satan was willing, "he could not prevail against one just man" and if it were possible, "he would not have asked permission", but as it is, he had to and this shows his lack of power.

Remember, "destruction would not have come even on his cattle had not God allowed it". Satan doesn't he have "the power over swine" since in the Gospels we see that Legion begged Jesus to release them into the herd of pigs![115]

> But if they had power not even against swine, much less have they any over men formed in the image of God.

And so, with all of this in mind, we ought to have only fear of God, and not of demons. Even if they come at us from all sides and intensify their attacks, all the more should we intensify our dedication to God and to prayer to combat the evil one, reminding ourselves of the words of our Saviour in Luke 10:19 –

---

115 *cf.* Matt 8:31

"Behold I have given to you power to tread upon serpents and scorpions, and upon all the power of the enemy!"

Amen!

Notes

DAY 24

ATHANASIUS: LIFE OF ANTHONY, CHAPS. 31–40

Today we continue with Anthony's exposition on the trickery and deceptions of demons who try to cause the faithful to stumble and be fooled by their power. You don't often hear much taught on this area of Christian spirituality these days, at least, not in the church circles I've been a part of in the last few years, and not in so much depth as you can read here via Anthony's teaching.

Even from my own various experiences with this type of thing, I can attest to what Anthony is teaching and explaining here, and it really goes to show the level of deception that demons bring. Athanasius is writing this biography nearly 1700 years or so ago, and yet the demonic trickery explained here is really no different than what I've seen myself in my own short lifetime — which really goes to show the weakness of the enemy and the lack of weapons he has to work with, if nothing has changed that much in all this time! Our Lord really is greater and stronger!

The Deception Of Demons

Anthony really draws on just how little power these evil forces have, but also explains how they can make themselves *seem* more powerful than they are. Just as in the chapters yesterday where he said that, like the Apostles, we must not be "ignorant of [the enemies] devices",[116] he now goes into more detail so that we may learn what these devices are, and no longer remain in ignorance.

---

116 *cf.* 2 Cor 2:11

Anthony goes on to explain something which is especially noteworthy concerning any prophetic utterances demons may give, and how it is possible that they can be accurate in what they foretell. I found this very interesting to read because it's exactly the way I understand how demons work from what the Lord revealed to me after I was delivered from the demonic many years ago.

Anthony also clarifies that only God knows the things which are unseen and so, we may be dazzled, or some may be marvelled at the foreknowledge of other spirits, but they are actually only *pretending* to know anything real about the future.

Giving an example from something Anthony and others have seemingly witnessed, he says that "often [the demons] announce beforehand that the brethren are coming days after. And they do come" — but they don't do this to benefit the believers, or because they care, no, they do this to gain trust so that in the long run they may destroy those who place their trust in the demons.

But How Do They Know What's Coming Before We Know It?

Anthony lays it our quite plainly:

> For what wonder is it, if with more subtle bodies than men have, when they have seen them start on their journey, they surpass them in speed, and announce

their coming? Just as a horseman getting a start of a man on foot announces the arrival of the latter beforehand, so in this there is no need for us to wonder at them.

Basically, the demons just see what is already in motion, no matter the spacial distance, and then announce it to others ahead of time so it has the appearance of prophecy. It is no different than when a man gets a higher perspective from a mountain top, or similar, to see things which are far off that are approaching in the distance.

> For they know nothing of themselves, but, like thieves, what they get to know from others they pass on, and guess at rather than foretell things. Therefore if sometimes they speak the truth, let no one marvel at them for this.

Just as those who study the weather, or doctors who study the body, get to know the symptoms and patterns so as to be able to predict with some accuracy what is happening before it does, no one would say these know this by inspiration, "but from experience and practice". It is in the same way that these demons also operate.

If we should we desire to know the future — desire to use the gifts of the Spirit, as Paul encouraged,[117] — then it should be through our discipline to God to keep ourselves pure so that when our "soul is perfectly pure

---

117 *cf.* 1 Cor 14:1,5

and in its natural state, it is able, being clear-sighted, to see more and further than the demons – for it has the Lord who reveals to it".

How Do We Distinguish Between The Good And The Evil?

Any deceiving spirit will flee at the sign of Christ:

> "When, therefore, they come by night to you and wish to tell the future, or say, "we are the angels," give no heed, for they lie … but rather sign yourselves [with the cross] … and pray, and you shall see them vanish."

But if they "shamelessly stand their ground", Anthony warns, then fear them not and don't think that they may be good spirits. "For the presence either of the good or evil by the help of God can easily be distinguished" — the evil comes with much fear and distraction on our minds so that we are not focussed right on God.

Good spirits from the Lord however, come "so quietly and gently that immediately joy, gladness and courage arise in the soul" since the Lord our God is ours, and their, joy and the "thoughts of the soul remain unruffled and undisturbed". Just as we see in Scripture, when the angels came to give messages, they started with "fear not" and removed all fear on those listening, despite being in the presence of God and powerful beings.

To discern the spirits is to do so as follows:

> If your fear is immediately taken away and in place of it comes joy unspeakable, cheerfulness, courage, renewed strength, calmness of thought ... then is it surely the Lord!

But, to the contrary:

> ...whenever the soul remains fearful there is a presence of the enemies. For the demons do not take away the fear of their presence as the great archangel Gabriel did for Mary and Zacharias.

Rebuking The Enemy

Just as Jesus rebuked the devil,[118] so we can also though the power of the Spirit within us.

In doing so, we must remember to not lift up those who cast out demons, or those who heal, as worthy of anything more than those who do not do these things. This should not be a point of pride for us which could make us stumble, "for the working of signs is not ours but the Saviour's work"; so we should keep in mind what Jesus said to his disciples on this matter:

Luke 10:20
Nevertheless, do not rejoice at this, that the spirits submit to you, but rejoice that your names are written in heaven.

---

118 *cf.* Matt 4:10

Those who boasted in their works rather than in Christ who has sealed them[119] were those who will be turned away by Jesus in judgement;[120] and so because of this, Anthony urges that we seek the gift of discernment as John wrote in his letter[121] that we may not be deceived.

Anthony goes on to give some of his personal testimony to show that he is not just speaking at random, but from experience and from what the Lord had shown him. From visions and visitations of demons in disguise as angels or monks to trick him, to appearances of soldiers and beasts to scare him, to physical beatings; he spoke the name of Christ, sang Psalms and kept himself in prayer, and the demons fled and disappeared "like smoke".

In all things he kept this one thing at the forefront of his mind, and we should too, whether it be demons we face, or human persecutions, this saying rings true:

Romans 8:3
Nothing shall separate me from the love of Christ

I hope this has encouraged you to stay strong in Christ whatever the circumstances.[122]

---

119 *cf.* 2 Cor 1:22; Eph 1:13; 4:30

120 *cf.* Matt 7:22

121 *cf.* 1 John 4:1

122 *cf.* Philippians 4: 11-13

Notes

Notes

DAY 25

ATHANASIUS: LIFE OF ANTHONY, CHAPS. 41–50

Today continues with a little more teaching and experience from Anthony on demons and the spiritual battle we are all in as believers.

This chapter opens with a strange anecdote from the time that Anthony was still living in his "cell" (the secluded room on the edge of the Nile, not a prison!).

"Once someone knocked at the door of my cell", he begins, and getting up to answer the door, he sees "one who seemed of great size and tall" standing there. Enquiring who this person was, he answered, "I am Satan". Unphased by this, Anthony just asks him what he is doing there at his door! Satan then just bemoans that all of the "monks and all other Christians" just blame him "undeservedly" and curse him "hourly", to which Anthony essentially asks him, *'then why do you bother them in the first place if you don't want to be blamed for it?'*.[123]

Satan then goes on to say that there's no point in cursing him so much since he doesn't have as much power as people think, and then goes on to quote Psalm 9 saying, "I have become weak. Have they not read [the Scriptures?]".

Psalms 9:6
The swords of the enemy have come to an end, and you have destroyed the cities?

---

123 Maybe this is what inspired the *Rolling Stones* song title "Sympathy for the Devil"? Sorry, no more puns.

"I have no longer a place, a weapon, a city. The Christians are spread everywhere", Satan goes on to explain. Anthony agrees with him, rejoicing that, "the coming of Christ has made you weak, and He has cast you down and stripped you"! But on mentioning the Lord's name, Satan vanished as he could not bear to be in the presence of even the name of Jesus.

So now, if even the devil himself confesses that he is weak and defeated, then we should no longer despair at demons, for we know their weakness, and can now despise them.

> Let us consider in our soul that the Lord is with us, who put the evil spirits to flight and broke their power. Let us consider and lay to heart that while the Lord is with us, our foes can do us no hurt.

Coming to a close on his teaching about evil spirits, Anthony gives us the simplest way in which we can test the spirits:

If a vision or apparition appears before you, don't lie down in fear, all you need do is ask, "who are you and from where do you come?". If the vision is a holy one, then like we see in the Scriptures, the angels will assure you and turn fear into joy. But if it is of evil origins, the fear remains and spirit may fumble with clever words of deception and trickery to hide it's purpose. Remain steadfast in your faith and purpose of mind with Christ and tell that demon to flee in the name of Jesus, and he will!

The Growth Of The Monastic Life At This Time (about 305 AD)

As Anthony taught on these things, the people rejoiced and came to despise the Evil One even more and became strengthened in their faith.

> So their cells were in the mountains, filled with holy bands of men who sang psalms, loved reading, fasted, prayed, rejoiced in the hope of things to come, laboured in almsgiving, and preserved love and harmony one with another.

More and more people came to saving faith and began living the ascetic lifestyle, to the point that there was hardly any wrongdoing committed in their area.

During this time, it seems as though Anthony became a little strange. With his focus so much on heaven and on the thought of eventually going to be fully spiritual with no need to support the body through food and drink, he withdrew from the other monks to be in solitude again, feeling shame for eating in front of them and trying to not to give into the pleasures of the body in any conceivable way.

Desire For Martyrdom At Alexandria During The Persecution (311 AD)

The Church came under persecution from Maximinus

II,[124] who took many Christians away to Alexandria to be martyred. Anthony, having not been caught, followed anyway hoping to either be a witness or to at least minister to those who had been taken, and ended up going to those in the mines and the prisons.

The judge who was overseeing the martyrs, saw this fearless zeal from Anthony and his companions, and "commanded that no monk should appear in the judgement hall, nor remain at all in the city" which led to many Christians going into hiding at that time.

Life After The Persecutions

After the persecutions ended, Anthony retreated back to his cell where he became a little depressed by the sound of things, and made his discipline more harsh on himself. After a while someone came to his door seeking his help through prayer for their daughter who had a demon.

But Anthony, not wanting to become puffed up, simply said that he is only a man like the visitor, and can do no more than he, but if he goes in faith in Christ, then he shall receive what he asks, quoting Luke 11:9. The daughter was freed from the evil spirit, and so more people came to sit at Anthony's door seeking help to be healed, though he wouldn't open the door to them. Though through their sincere prayers and

---

124 Maximinus renewed the persecution of Christians after various urban authorities put pressure on him to expel Christians from their cities.

faith, they were healed, and the Lord did "many other things also through Anthony".

Anthony Seeks Another Place

Since so many people were gathered around Anthony's cell seeking for his help and prayers, and because he didn't want to get prideful due to the signs that the Lord was doing through him, he decided to find a new place to dwell.

So he set off to find a new secluded place and, by a heavenly voice, was pointed towards a group of Saracens[125] who were heading deeper into the desert; so Anthony travelled with them for three days and three nights until he came to a new mountain with a clear, fresh stream and a plain with some palm trees. It was here that he decided to settle down to stay.

Tomorrow we will see how Anthony gets on at his new home and what the Lord does with him there! I hope you're finding the life of Anthony as interesting as I am and look forward to what comes next.

---

125 In Medieval Latin, this term had become synonymous with "Muslim"; but pre-12th century it simply referred to groups of people who lived in desert areas.

Notes

DAY 26

ATHANASIUS: LIFE OF ANTHONY, CHAPS. 51–60

Today we pick up at the start of a new chapter in Anthony's life. He's just relocated to a new mountain farther into the Egyptian desert with the aid of the Saracens. Anthony was moved to love the area he found with what is described as a 'divine love' that helped him to settle there. But it soon became a small burden to him as people would seek him out and look to visit him, or to bring him bread. This area was a three day and night trek from where he previously lived, so the thought of other people taking this treacherous journey concerned him dearly. Eventually, after asking some monks to bring him corn and seeds, he managed to till the ground to be able to make his own bread and grow his own herbs to save others from needing to bring him food.

Sometimes the wild animals would ruin his garden looking for food and water, but at one point Anthony gently captured an animal and said to it, "Why do you hurt me, when I hurt none of you? Depart, and in the name of the Lord come not nigh this spot" and as though they could understand his words, no longer did the animals come back!

Not Against Flesh And Blood

By this point in time, Anthony was an old man and some of the other believers who had served him, would bring olives and oil and other supplies once a month. Upon visiting him they would sometimes witness strange things going on as spiritual events formed against Anthony, as though soldiers and beasts were attacking him, but he would be seen praying against them and the demons fleeing.

They saw and heard "tumults, many voices, and, as it were, the clash of arms ... and [Anthony] also fighting as though against visible beings" since he wrestled not against 'flesh and blood' "but against opposing demons". Athanasius learned these things from those who visited Anthony during these times.

At other times, demons would make appearances to try and bring fear and to shake his trust in Christ, or they would cause all the hyenas nearby to come and surround Anthony. But, not fearing the Evil One and having his mind set on Christ, he rebuked them and commanded that hey leave in the name of the Lord if they were sent by demons, which they did and he was then left alone.

Anthony Visits The Other Monks

Some time later, the other monks came and enquired of Anthony, wanting him to come and visit them at their mountain, so he set off on the journey back with those who came to see him. On their way through the desert, their water ran out and they were still some way from any water source, and so the men despaired and let their camel go, and sat on the ground unable to move. Anthony, seeing the danger, went a short walk away to pray to the Lord for help, and immediately, water sprang up where he was standing! So they filled their bottles, found the camel and went on their way refreshed and restored.

On arriving at the the cells of the other monks, Anthony rejoiced in seeing their earnestness and was also happy to find that his sister had become the leader of the nuns in her old age.

During this time, Anthony gave some teaching to the monks and hermits living there, on his guidelines for the discipline he'd developed:

> Believe on the Lord and love Him; keep yourselves from filthy thoughts and fleshly pleasures, and as it is written in the Proverbs, be not deceived "by the fullness of the belly." Pray continually; avoid vainglory; sing psalms before sleep and on awaking; hold in your heart the commandments of Scripture; be mindful of the works of the saints that your souls being put in remembrance of the commandments may be brought into harmony with the zeal of the saints.

He also encouraged them to live by the words of Paul in Ephesians 4:26, where he said not to let the sun go down on your anger. Anthony interpreted this further to mean not just anger, but any sin which was committed, so that before the end of the day you have to set things right with others or have prayed and repented to the Lord. Even further still, he would teach that in order to control our thoughts so that we let nothing sinful enter our mind (i.e. *"take every thought captive"* — 2 Cor 10:5), that the monks should write down every thought they have as though they were to read them out loud to one another at the end of the day. Through seeing what we think and with the idea of others knowing it, the shame ought to keep us in check and help to strengthen our minds against evil thoughts, "thus fashioning ourselves we shall be able to keep the body in subjection, to please the Lord, and to trample on the devices of the enemy".

Miracles Of Healing That The Lord Did Through Anthony

Anthony would spend a lot of his time praying with those who suffered, and sometimes those with illnesses would receive healing. But he taught not to boast if they were, and not to mutter if they weren't, but to rejoice in all things and to be patient because "healing belonged neither to him nor to man at all, but only to the Lord" and God would do good to those he chose, when he chose to, and "those who were healed were taught not to give thanks to Anthony but to God alone".

At one time, a man named Fronto, an Officer of the Court, came to Anthony with a terrible disease where he would "to bite his own tongue and was in danger of injury to his eyes" and sought prayer. On seeing him, Anthony sent him away saying that on his departure he would be healed. But the man remained for a few days, so Anthony went again to him and told him that he wouldn't get what he wanted until he went on his way back to Egypt, so the man left and upon seeing Egypt, suddenly he received his healing as Anthony had said, "which the Saviour had revealed to him in prayer".

Another time a woman from Busiris Tripolitania came to him who was paralysed and had strange fluid issues coming from her eyes, nose and ears. Her parents had heard of Anthony and because they had read the Gospels of when Jesus healed the woman who had been bleeding for many years, they took her to the monk seeking prayer for healing too. On arriving at the place where the monks were staying, some of Anthony's companions went to find him and tell him about the girl, but on coming to him, he already knew about her and her condition. He told them to go back to the girl and they will find her healed, since "the accomplishment of this is not mine, that she should come to me, wretched man that I am, but her healing is the work of the Saviour". Anthony always made sure to place the glory where it belonged and never to take any credit for himself in these things.

At another time, two monks were travelling through the desert, and their water supplies ran dry. One of them died and the other was on the brink of death when it was revealed to Anthony during prayer that this was happening — so he sent two men to that location with water to save the monk!

One other time when Anthony was sitting and praying, he looked up and saw a man in a vision, being taken upwards towards many who were joyful at his arrival. Wondering what this was, he prayed and enquired of the Lord, who responded by telling him it was the soul of "Amun, the monk at Nitria" being taken up into the presence of the Father, for he had died. The companions of Anthony, seeing the amazed expression on his face, asked what he was seeing, and he explained that Amun had died. This monk lived about thirteen days travel away and was well known to the monks where Anthony was staying.

Amun had often stayed with them, and was known for the signs which the Lord had performed through him as well. One of these signs, which is recollected here by Athanasius, was of a time when Amun had to cross a river called Lycus with a companion of his. To avoid the shame of seeing the other naked while swimming, Amun went first while his friend, Theodorus, stayed a little distance away. But he became afraid of having to become naked, even of seeing himself that way, that while pondering on this and how he should approach the situation, he suddenly found himself on the other side of the river standing by Amun!

If that wasn't surprising enough, he noticed that Amun wasn't even wet and so he asked how it was possible, but Amun refused to tell him. Theodorus grabbed his feet and wouldn't let him go until he explained it, so Amun swore him to secrecy until after his death and told him that he had not even touched the water as the Lord had carried him across the river in a similar way that Jesus allowed Peter to walk on water. Now that Amun had died, Theodorus recalled the story to the other monks.

About thirty days later, some men from Nitria

arrived to tell the news of the death of Amun, and those who met them enquired of the time of death and saw that it was at the very moment when Anthony had seen the vision from the Lord, and they all marvelled and rejoiced at the things the Lord did through Anthony.

That's all from today's reading, but *wow* what a lot to take in! The Lord surely did some amazing things through his servant Anthony, which in turn caused many to come to faith after hearing about his reputation for his dedication to the Lord and the wonders which were worked through him.

I hope this inspires you to seek the Lord more and to persevere with your faith and the discipline of living as Jesus commanded us, and as the Apostles taught us via their letters.

Notes

DAY 27

ATHANASIUS: LIFE OF ANTHONY, CHAPS. 61-70

Here we begin with a couple more examples of the healing miracles which were worked through Anthony, which carry over from yesterday's chapters. Many people would travel from far and wide to see and hear Anthony, to receive prayer for sickness or for freedom from demons; but he "used to ask that no one should wonder at him for this; but should rather marvel at the Lord for having granted to us men to know Him as far as our powers extended."

Two examples are given of demonic possession, the first was when Anthony was asked to visit some monks on a boat. On arriving, there was a stench so bad in that place that Anthony said it was unusual and not natural. The people on board just said it was due to the cargo of meat, but as Anthony preached, a boy in the crowd yelled out and Anthony rebuked the demon in him, setting the boy free and with it, the stench left. The other time was about an official who had been possessed so badly that he would not know where he went and ate his own excrement! The man somehow ended up by Anthony one day, so he sat and prayed with him all night until the demon finally let go and left with a violent outburst.

Athanasius breaks here to make a note that many monks had "related with the greatest agreement and unanimity that many other such like things were done" through Anthony, and these things recalled here were like highlights to his life story.

Anthony's Vision About Forgiveness Of Sins

Athanasius relates now of a time when Anthony was praying and about to go and eat. On standing up he suddenly found himself in the Spirit and in what we'd probably call an 'out of body experience' in today's language. Suddenly he was taken up into the air by "certain ones", which I assume to mean angels because he is then opposed by "certain bitter and terrible beings" which would seem to describe something like demons. They try to stop his passage by accusing him of his sins, but the ones accompanying Anthony tell them that, "the Lord has wiped out the sins from his birth" but that only since the time he became a monk can they accuse him; they failed and Anthony was allowed to pass.

Suddenly Anthony found himself back in his body as before, and was astonished at "what mighty opponents our wrestling" is against, and recalled what Paul taught in his epistles about our battles being against the "ruler of the power of the air".[126] So he taught all the more passionately about the need to put on the whole armour of God[127] and for living right before God so that the enemy may not have anything evil to say against us.[128]

---

126 Eph 2:2

127 *cf.* Eph 6:13

128 *cf.* Titus 2:8

Anthony's Vision On The Passing Of Souls

At another time when Anthony was praying at night, after a discussion with some people about what happens to the soul after death, he heard a voice from above telling him to go outside and look up.

On going, he saw a giant being going up as tall as the clouds, and people ascending upwards through the clouds. Some of the people were being hindered while others flew by without issue. He had his mind opened to understand what he was seeing, and it was explained that the giant was the enemy stopping those souls from heading to heaven who were accountable to the devil but those who belonged to God could pass by without issue.

Anthony Against Heretics And Heresy, Such As Arianism

When schisms and heresies arose, such as the Meletian[129] schismatics, or the Manichæan heretics,[130] Anthony would have no part of it nor would be even meet with them except to try and have them convert to

---

129 Meletius, Bishop of Lycopolis in Egypt, was removed from is office around 306 AD for sacrificing to idols amongst other things.

130 Manichæism is a religion founded in the latter half of the third century by a Persian named Mani. It is a form of religious Dualism mixed together with various aspects of other religions, such as: Zoroastrian Dualism, Babylonian folklore, Buddhist ethics and superficial Christian elements.

the truth.

He also despised the Arians and their heresy, and warned that none should go near them nor hold to their belief. At one point, certain "madmen", who were Arians, came to Anthony so that he could learn more about their doctrine, but he drove them away saying their "words were worse than the poison of serpents" when he understood more about what they taught!

After this, some more Arians went about and lied saying that Anthony agreed with their doctrine. On hearing this, all of the bishops and other brethren summoned Anthony to Alexandria to be questioned about it. He denounced the heresy as something antichrist and defended the divinity of Christ, saying,

> …the Son of God was not a created being, neither had He come into being from non-existence, but that He was the Eternal Word and Wisdom of the Essence of the Father. And therefore it was impious to say, 'there was a time when He was not,' for the Word was always co-existent with the Father. Wherefore have no fellowship with the most impious Arians. For there is no communion between light and darkness. (2 Corinthians 6:14)

He goes on to teach that they, and anyone who denies Christ's divinity and says that he is a created being, are no better than the heathen, "since they worship that which is created" rather than "the Creator, the Lord of all, by whom all things came into being, with those things which were originated".[131]

On hearing that Anthony had denounced the Arians, the city rejoiced and even the Greeks and their temple priests came to see Anthony speak, and in that time many people were healed and set free from demons, and "as many became Christians in those few days as one would have seen made in a year"!

That must have been quite some party with all those people coming to Christ and worshipping him, what a sight it must have been. I pray that God convicts us all to live a more pious life and to raise up men and women of God who will change cities with the Gospel as Anthony did!

---

131 *cf.* John 1:1-4

Notes

DAY 28

ATHANASIUS: LIFE OF ANTHONY, CHAPS. 71–80

Well here we are at the penultimate reading before we read the end of this biography and move on from the *Life of Anthony*.

Today we see the ways in which the Greek philosophers would come and listen to Anthony speak and how they would sometimes discuss things with him, or at other times would mock him and the message of the Cross. They came to mock Anthony because he had never "learned letters" and was unable to read or write, so the Greeks thought he would be an unkempt and ignorant man, reared in the mountains and unable to reason properly.

Anthony Vs Greek Philosophers

At one time during an event, Anthony noticed there were two Greek philosophers present (due to the way they were dressed), and so he approached them asking them why did they "come to a foolish man", to which they said they didn't think he was foolish, but "exceedingly prudent" — meaning: *"wise; having or showing acute mental discernment"* — so the Greeks recognised that Anthony wasn't just some mountain-dwelling bumpkin!

Anthony responds to the philosophers by using their Greek logic against them, by saying that if they thought him foolish, then their journey would be a wasted effort, but since they think he is prudent, and since they would agree that we should imitate that which is good, then therefore they ought to imitate him if they wish to also be prudent. Since it was they who sought out Anthony, then they should become as he was, i.e. a Christian. "But they departed with wonder, for they saw that even demons feared Anthony".

Another time some more Greek philosophers came to mock Anthony for his lack of learning with regards to reading and writing. So he asked them, "which is first, mind or letters?" to which they obviously replied, "mind", saying it was "the inventor of letters". So Anthony said to them that whoever has "a sound mind hath not need of letters" and at this they marvelled at him since he reasoned so well despite his appearance and lack of education from living in the mountains.

Philosophers Try To Mock The Cross

At another time, some more Greek philosophers came and tried to mock the beliefs of the Christians for the preaching of the cross, which as we know from Scripture, is not something unexpected.[132] On hearing their objections, Anthony answered them by turning their own beliefs against them;

> Which is more beautiful, to confess the Cross or to attribute to those whom you call gods adultery and the seduction of boys? [...] Next, which is better, to say that the Word of God was not changed, but, being the same, He took a human body for the salvation and well-being of man, that having shared in human birth He might make man partake in the divine and spiritual nature; or to liken the divine to senseless animals and

132 *cf.* 1 Cor 1:18

consequently to worship four-footed beasts, creeping things and the likenesses of men? For these things, are the objects of reverence of you wise men. But how do you dare to mock us, who say that Christ has appeared as man...

He goes on to say that they talk endlessly about "the wanderings of Osiris and Isis, the plots of Typhon, the flight of Cronos, his eating his children and the slaughter of his father" as their form of wisdom, yet mock the cross but marvel at the resurrection! But "the same men who told us of the [resurrection] wrote [about the cross]", Anthony responds. They would mock the cross but be then are silent about all the miracles and wonders which Jesus did which show that "Christ is no longer a man but God"; so they do themselves "much injustice" to have not read the Scriptures properly in order that they should see that "the deeds of Christ prove Him to be God come upon earth for the salvation of men".

Since they allegorise all of creation with the Greek legends of Poseidon, Apollo, Artemis etc., they "do not worship God Himself, but serve the creature rather than God who created all things" and "make gods of the things created" instead of giving the rightful honour to the "master builder" who is the Creator of all things; and at this, Anthony silenced his opponents.[133]

---

133 *cf.* 2 Cor 10: 4-5

Anthony's Critics Silenced

He continued to preach the message of the Cross to them though: "Tell us therefore where your oracles are now? Where are the charms of the Egyptians? Where the delusions of the magicians? When did all these things cease and grow weak except when the Cross of Christ arose?"

He argues that if by the rising of the cross and the death of Christ put an end to all these powers,[134] then how is it something to be mocked, surely the only things worthy of mockery now are those powers which have been disarmed. For in every city, "our side flourishes and multiplies over yours" despite the persecutions and mockery Christians receive. Even though the Greek legends are honoured everywhere, their followers diminish and their faith perishes, yet the Christians, even though killed by kings, flourishes all the more! As Tertullian[135] is recorded as saying, which relates to this, *"the blood of the martyrs are the seed of the Church"*!

These signs, Anthony argues, are the proof of our faith. Proof doesn't lie in fancy, well-worded arguments, as the Greeks would have it or want, but rather in the manifestation of faith. To which, Anthony pointed out, that in their midst were some who were

---

134 *cf.* Col 2:15

135 Tertullian (c. 155–240 AD) is known as "the father of Latin theology" and "the founder of Western theology". Most of his writing was in defence of the Faith against persecution and heresy.

"vexed with demons"; so they had them brought before him. He goes on to say that with all their wordy arguments, magic, arts or idols, they cannot cleanse such a person. So "put away your strife with us and you shall see the power of the Cross of Christ" he declares before praying for these people, signing them with the cross a few times and then calling upon Christ, to which they got up whole and were totally healed and now free of the demons!

The Greek philosophers "were astonished exceedingly at the understanding of the man and at the sign which had been wrought", but Anthony rebuked them saying "we are not the doers of these things, but it is Christ who worketh them by means of those who believe on Him" and called on them to believe in Jesus. But they "saluted him and departed, confessing the benefit they had received from him".

What is sad, is that I've seen so many times the power of God at work in people's lives like this similar to these Greek philosophers, yet even though they have recognised and acknowledged God in it, they still do as the Greeks did and just "salute and depart". They take the blessing but refuse to change their lives and follow Christ, being in some sense the fulfilment of the *Parable of the Sower*[136] as people who are like the seed on the path or rocky ground.

Tomorrow we conclude with Athanasius' biography of Anthony and see what he did in his final years.

---

136 *cf.* Matt 13:1-9

Notes

DAY 29

ATHANASIUS: LIFE OF ANTHONY, CHAPS. 81-94

Here we are at the end of the *Life of Anthony* in the final chapters of Athanasius' biography, and the final chapters of Anthony's life at the grand old age of **105**! By this point in his life he had become widely renowned and respected far and wide, so much that judges and rulers would come and seek his advice on things, or sought out encouragement in their own faith. Many looked up to Anthony as a father figure, even the emperor Constantine Augustus, and his sons Constantius and Constans the Augusti, who "wrote letters to him, as to a father, and begged an answer from him" since they themselves had come to the faith. Despite rulers and kings writing to him and seeking his advice, Anthony thought nothing of it and didn't allow himself to become puffed up with pride over the status of men.

After meeting and seeing the various people who would visit, Anthony would retreat to the "inner mountain" where he resided and spent much of his time in prayer. It was here that those who accompanied him would often see that Anthony was "wrapped in a vision" and would not speak or move.

Anthony Foresees Persecution

At one time while Anthony was working, he fell into a trance with loud groans and trembling. Those who were with him were "trembling and terrified" and sought to learn from him what it was that he saw; after a while, Anthony explained that persecution was coming upon the Church from the Arian heretics.

Athanasius interjects here to say that two years after Anthony saw these things, the "plunder of the churches took place, when [the Arians] violently carried off the vessels" from the churches along with "the heathens" who they also conscripted to help them. But Anthony encouraged his brothers and told them that things would be put right and everything would be restored in the end, and to avoid the teaching of the Arians in the meantime, "for their teaching is not that of the Apostles, but that of demons and their father the devil".

How Anthony Was Used By The Lord

Here it is stated that although many great signs and wonders were done through the hands of Anthony, he never let this go to his head and always pointed to Christ as the reason and source of all the wonders. He would often teach on faith from the words of Jesus — that if you have only faith the size of a mustard seed, you can move mountains and that nothing shall be impossible,[137] and that if you ask the Father for anything in the name of Jesus, it shall be given,[138] such as casting out demons, healing the sick and raising the dead.[139]

He taught this way so that when he prayed for people, he "healed not by commanding, but by prayer and speaking the name of Christ. So that it was clear to

---

137 *cf.* Matt 17:20

138 *cf.* John 16:23

139 *cf.* Matt 10:8

all that it was not he himself who worked, but the Lord who showed mercy by his means and healed the sufferers".

Persecutions From Arian Sympathisers

At another point, a General Balacius came against the Christians who didn't hold to the Arian view of Jesus (the doctrine which states that the Son had a beginning and wasn't eternally with the Father with no beginning). He was so ruthless that he "beat virgins, and stripped and scourged monks"! Anthony took it upon himself to write to this man with a prophetic warning telling him to cease his persecutions, otherwise wrath would come on him very shortly since "it is on the point of coming upon" him already. He ignore the warning, and only eight days later, died from an unusual horse riding accident where one of his regular steeds, which was known to be a mild-mannered and temperate horse, suddenly bucked him off and bit through his leg which led to his death.

This served as a warning to all who were cruel or who may have planned to inflict punishment on the Christians, and many people sought out Anthony to hear him speak, or to receive prayer, with a lot of people turning from their worldly ways and dedicating themselves to the monastic life.

The Death Of Anthony

Anthony had learned "from Providence" (meaning either he learned it from God or just felt it was close because he was 105 years old), that his end was near and so he went out to see the monks in the "outer mountain" to bid them farewell and give them one last exhortation before he left them, "as though sailing from a foreign city to his own". He encouraged them to remember all that he taught them, to keep in the discipline and to "observe the traditions of the fathers, and chiefly the holy faith in our Lord Jesus Christ, which you have learned from the Scripture". The monks "wept, and embraced, and kissed the old man" and he advised them on how to bury him, since the Egyptians liked to wrap their dead and display revered men in their homes as a display. Anthony instructed them that since Jesus was buried in the ground, that that was the only proper way to treat the dead; not to display them.

So he left for the inner mountain where he had his two companions promise to bury him secretly, and then he lay down and died with a smile upon his face, "as though he saw friends coming to him and was glad because of them".

Athanasius closes his record of Anthony's life by praising the type of life he lived and how he lived it purely for God from his youth.

This is the end of Anthony's life in the body and the above was the beginning of the discipline. Even if this account is small compared with his merit, still from this reflect how great Anthony, the man of God, was. [...] Read these words, therefore, to the rest of the brethren that they may learn what the life of monks ought to be; and may believe that our Lord and Saviour Jesus Christ glorifies those who glorify Him. ... Amen

I feel like I'm parting ways with an old friend after reading about St. Anthony in so much detail over these last few days. His life story has definitely had an impact on me and it has given me things to consider, and areas in my life to look where I want to be more disciplined. I pray the same for anyone else who reads this biography.

Notes

DAY 30

CYRIL OF JERUSALEM: CATECHETICAL LECTURES: LECTURE XIX

Who: Bishop of Jerusalem and Doctor of the Church,[140] born about 315 AD; died 386 AD. Little is known of his life, except from some information gathered from his younger contemporaries: Epiphanius, Jerome, and Rufinus; as well as from the fifth-century historians, Socrates, Sozomen and Theodoret.

What: Each of the lectures deal with a different topic to teach converts the mysteries of the Church, particularly: rites of the renunciation of Satan and his works, of anointing with oil, of baptism, of anointing with the holy chrism,[141] and of partaking of the body and blood of Christ.

Why: Cyril delivered to new converts five lectures "On the Mysteries", in which he explains the rites by which they have been admitted to fellowship in the church, after they had been baptised.

When: Around 348-350 AD

---

140 This was a title given to certain people on account of the great advantage the whole Church has obtained from their doctrine.

141 Chrism, also called myrrh. A holy anointing and consecrated oil used in the administration of certain sacraments. It is still used today in various older denominations.

Today we begin a new series of texts to read by Cyril of Jerusalem. He actually wrote lots of lectures to teach new converts (23 in total), but we're only beginning with lecture nineteen where he begins to teach on certain "mysteries" of the Church — such as anointing with oil, the Eucharist and renouncing Satan amongst others.

These lectures were given after people had been baptised into the faith and were undergoing what is called "catechism", which basically means, *'a summary of the principles of Christian religion in the form of questions and answers, used for religious instruction.'*[142]

This lecture we're looking at today is on the renouncing of Satan and turning from worldly things, in order to be focused on Christ now instead. Each catechism is based on a passage of Scripture, this one is on 1 Peter 5:8-14, specifically, verses 8 and 9:

> Discipline yourselves, keep alert. Like a roaring lion your adversary the devil prowls around, looking for someone to devour. Resist him, steadfast in your faith, for you know that your brothers and sisters in all the world are undergoing the same kinds of suffering.

Cyril recounts how that when they went into the baptistery, they were instructed to "stretch forth [their] hand, and as in the presence of Satan [they] renounced

---

142 Dictionary definition, retrieved from: *https://en.oxforddictionaries.com/definition/catechism*

him", and then proceeds to break down each of the different statements which the baptised have to declare. This practice is contrasted with Moses who was sent by God to Egypt, and with Christ who was sent by the Father to the world, and how the Hebrews put lamb's blood on their door posts to be delivered from the destroyer. Now Christ as the perfect lamb, sacrificed himself to rescue those oppressed under sin with his own blood.

Now Turn From The Old To The New, From The Figure To The Reality

The old, in Moses, prefigured the new, in Christ, who is the reality we now live in. The enemy of old in the person of Pharaoh, chased the Hebrews to the sea, and even through it, but was engulfed when it closed in around him now prefigures what happens in baptism:

> The tyrant of old was drowned in the sea; and this present one disappears in the water of salvation.

Personally, I really like that analogy of baptism consuming Satan and washing him out of our lives. I've never heard it put quite that way before.

The phrases which the converts have to recite remind me of the liturgy which you have to say during a Christening. That in itself shows an interesting link to how this tradition and practice has been preserved in certain churches.

I'll contrast the two just to show the similarities; I'm using the Anglican baptism liturgy[143] since that's what I'm most familiar with from memory from growing up in the Church of England:

> Do you reject the devil and all rebellion against God?
> *I reject them.*
>
> Do you renounce the deceit and corruption of evil?
> *I renounce them.*
>
> Do you repent of the sins that separate us from God and neighbour?
> *I repent of them.*
>
> Do you turn to Christ as Saviour?
> *I turn to Christ.*
>
> Do you submit to Christ as Lord?
> *I submit to Christ.*
>
> Do you come to Christ, the way, the truth and the life?
> *I come to Christ.*

And this is the text from Cyril's lecture which I've compiled into one paragraph of liturgy for easier reading:

> I renounce thee, Satan
> and all thy works.
> And all his pomp,
> and all thy service.

143 Anglican baptism liturgy — *https://www.churchofeng-land.org/prayer-worship/worship/texts/initiation/baptism.aspx*

I believe in the Father, and in the Son, and in the Holy Ghost, and in one Baptism of repentance.

Cyril expounds on each sentence to explain more about what each means and what it is they renounce and give up.

Satan and his works — Renouncing and turning from evil and sin.

All his pomp — From being involved in worldly affairs, such as "the madness of theatres, and horseraces, and hunting" and from "things which are hung up at idol festivals, either meat or bread, or other such things polluted by the invocation of the unclean spirits".

All thy service — From taking part in "idol temples; things done in honour of lifeless idols [...] The watching of birds, divination, omens, or amulets, or charms written on leaves, sorceries, or other evil arts"

I believe... — A way to symbolise and declare the turning from "West to East", from darkness to light. Now through the "holy Laver[144] of regeneration God has wiped away every tear from off all faces" by their regeneration in Christ.

---

144 The sacred wash bowl for the priests in the temple (Exodus 30:18; Exodus 30:28; Exodus 40:30, etc.). In this instance it's likely speaking of the baptistry pool in the church building. See: *http://www.biblestudytools.com/dictionary/laver/*

This is the end of this lecture, and from the way Cyril concludes, it sounds like each one of these lectures on the mysteries lead the converts one step at a time into "the Holy of Holies" of the full knowledge of the Church.

Tomorrow's lecture looks into Baptism itself, and the mystery of being baptised into Christ's death and resurrection. Exciting times ahead!

Notes

Notes

DAY 31

CYRIL OF JERUSALEM: CATECHETICAL LECTURES: LECTURE XX

Today's lecture on the mysteries by Cyril, is on baptism and is an exposition based on Romans 6:3-14.

Romans 6:3, 14
Do you not know that all of us who have been baptized into Christ Jesus were baptized into his death? … since you are not under law but under grace.

Now, these people that Cyril was teaching had already gone through the act of baptism, so now he was going over the symbolism and realities of what that meant to them personally.

In describing the baptism rite to make one of his points, Cyril gives us a small insight into how the Church in the fourth century performed this, which I always find interesting to see how things have changed or stayed the same over the centuries.

Before entering the waters, the one being baptised would strip of their tunic, symbolising "putting off the old man with his deeds"[145] and would then be naked as Christ was naked on the cross. In doing this they may no longer pick up the old garment any more, meaning to old self not the physical tunic, "which waxes corrupt in the lusts of deceit".[146]

O wondrous thing! You were naked in the sight of all, and were not ashamed; for truly ye bore the likeness of the first-formed Adam, who was naked in the garden,

145 *cf.* Col 3:9
146 *cf.* Eph 4:22

and was not ashamed.

After this, they were anointed with oil from head to toe, to symbolise being "cut off from the wild olive-tree, and grafted into the good one" Jesus Christ. During this time of anointing they are cleansed "by the invocation of God and by prayer, as not only to burn and cleanse away the traces of sins, but also to chase away all the invisible powers of the evil one".

Next, being led to the baptismal pool as Christ was carried from the cross to the tomb, they make their declaration of faith and are baptised three times in the name of the Father, Son and Holy Spirit. Three times in the water as Christ was three days in the grave. Though we don't really die, nor get buried, nor get resurrected in that moment physically, "our imitation was in a figure, and our salvation in reality", Cyril explains.

Like many other early church writers, Cyril views baptism as a way in which our sins are washed away, probably due to passages like Acts 2:38 (*"...so that your sins may be forgiven; and you will receive the gift of the Holy Spirit"*) and 2 Peter 3:21 ("*And baptism, which this prefigured, now saves you — not as a removal of dirt from the body, but as an appeal to God for a good conscience..."*).

So Cyril writes that baptism "purges our sins, and ministers to us the gift of the Holy Ghost" and is our part in the sufferings of Christ, recalling what Paul says in Romans 6:3 that we are "baptised into his death".

But he makes a point of emphasis that whilst these are symbols and figures of what happens to us during baptism, that Christ actually was crucified, died, was buried and rose again in reality; "in your case there was only a likeness of death and sufferings, whereas of salvation there was not a likeness but a reality".

Remember these things, he says, and keep them at the forefront of your mind because it is God who has presented you as alive from the dead.[147]

After reading all of this, it just reinforces my own conviction on how important baptism is, but also how misunderstood it can be, or how flippant it is sometimes presented in certain churches or denominations today.

Maybe some type of catechism/teaching course on what baptism means should still be taught in churches beforehand to new Christians, similar to how evangelical-type churches have the *Alpha Course*[148] to teach an overview of Christian doctrine.

Other than Anglicans, Roman Catholics (and other more traditional denominations, like Lutherans and Eastern Orthodox etc.), who still have a form of catechesis for baptism — Anglicans and Catholics call

147 *cf.* Rom 6:13

148 Alpha is a series of interactive sessions that freely explore the basics of the Christian faith — *http://alpha.org*

it "Confirmation", other *'newer'* denominations don't really have anything like this, and baptism is a lot more casual. It just seems to me that something so important and transformative should have a little more teaching and explanation before someone enters into it.

Paul spends a lot of his time teaching on the spirituality of baptism and how it relates us to Christ in a physical and spiritual way, and how this is pretty much the moment in which we are saved or regenerated and become the new creation. The early church seemed to grasp the magnitude of this, and maybe it's time our less traditional churches did so again?

Notes

Notes

DAY 32

CYRIL OF JERUSALEM: CATECHETICAL LECTURES: LECTURE XXI

Today's lecture on the mysteries by Cyril, is on "chrism"[149] and is an exposition based on 1 John 2:20-28.

> **1 John 2:20, 28**
> But you have been anointed by the Holy One … that when he is revealed we may have confidence and not be put to shame before him at his coming.

This was a new one to me when I first read this. I've never come across the word *chrism* before. From the passage of Scripture this lecture is based on, I guessed it was something to do with anointing, and on looking it up I found that it's actually a type of oil used in baptism: "a mixture of oil of olives and balsam".[150] Roman Catholics still use it today too for anointing the sick and in baptism.[151]

What Cyril describes in this lecture is the practice of anointing the recently baptised with this special oil as a sign of the Holy Spirit's sealing upon them, since they have "put on Christ"[152] and are adopted as sons[153]

---

149 Chrism, also called myrrh. A holy anointing and consecrated oil used in the administration of certain sacraments. It is still used today in various older denominations. See: *http://www.newadvent.org/cathen/03696b.htm*

150 Morrisroe, Patrick. "Chrism." The Catholic Encyclopedia. Vol. 3. New York: Robert Appleton Company, 1908. 23 Nov. 2017 <http://www.newadvent.org/cathen/03696b.htm>.

151 "What is chrism" — *http://www.uscatholic.org/articles/201606/what-chrism-30688*

152 *cf.* Gal 3:27

153 *cf.* Eph 1:5

and are now partakers of Christ also.[154]

Because Jesus was "in reality crucified, and buried, and raised" and they, in baptism, were also partakers in this figuratively. Likewise when Jesus was baptised and then anointed by the Holy Spirit, so now these catechumen were also partakers in Christ by being anointed by the oil symbolically as the Holy Spirit on them.[155]

"But beware of supposing this to be plain ointment", Cyril says, since after it is prayed over, "this holy ointment is no more simple ointment" — much like the bread of the Eucharist no longer stays as *just* bread after similar prayers.

So in the Eucharist, there is the *Real Presence* of Christ, and in Chrism there is the "real presence" of the Holy Spirit? I haven't heard of that aspect or teaching on a a Real Presence type of doctrine before so I find this to be an interesting insight to early beliefs.

Your Body Is Anointed With The Visible Ointment, Your Soul Is Sanctified By The Holy And Life-giving Spirit

Here, Cyril gives us a very interesting insight into how the early church anointed new believers:

---

154 *cf.* Heb 3:14

155 *cf.* Isa. 61:1; Acts 10:38

"And you were first anointed on the forehead..."
— this was to symbolise removing the shame of the first man, so that we "with unveiled faces" can be "transformed into the same image" of the Lord.[156]

"Then on your ears…" — this was to symbolise the opening of their ears to God's voice as Isaiah said in Isa. 50:4 *("Morning by morning he ... wakens my ear")* and as Jesus also declared Matt 11:15: "He that has ears to hear let him hear".

"Then on the nostrils…" — this was to symbolise what Paul wrote in 2 Cor 2:15: "we are the aroma of Christ".

"Afterwards on your breast…" — this was to be the "breastplate of righteousness"[157] so we are able to stand against the "wiles of the devil".[158]

Then after this was done, and having been "counted worthy" to receive this anointing, they are then "called Christians" living up to the name through their new birth.

Cyril goes on to explain how this type of anointing was prefigured in the Old Testament through Moses

---

156 *cf.* 2 Cor 3:18

157 *cf.* Eph 6:14; 1 Thess 5:8

158 *cf.* Eph 6:11

"bathing [Aaron] in water, he anointed him ... and made him High-priest".

> To them however these things happened in a figure, but to you not in a figure, but in truth; because you were truly anointed by the Holy Ghost. Christ is the beginning of your salvation

Cyril closes this lecture by encouraging his students to remain "unblemished" in this gift, pressing on in the good works of the Spirit, "for this holy thing is a spiritual safeguard of the body, and salvation of the soul".

Very interesting indeed! Baptism seemed like a much more involved process back in Cyril's day, compared with how things are often done today, which really ensured that the one being baptised understood what they were entering into.

Notes

Notes

DAY 33

CYRIL OF JERUSALEM: CATECHETICAL LECTURES: LECTURE XXII

Today's lecture on the mysteries by Cyril, is on the Body and Blood of Christ and is an exposition based on 1 Cor 11:23-25.

1 Cor 11:23-25
For I received from the Lord what I also handed on to you, that the Lord Jesus on the night when he was betrayed took a loaf of bread, and when he had given thanks, he broke it and said, "This is my body that is for you. Do this in remembrance of me." In the same way he took the cup also, after supper, saying, "This cup is the new covenant in my blood. Do this, as often as you drink it, in remembrance of me."

This whole lecture is about the Eucharist and it goes into some details about what happens spiritually during it, which will probably offend certain Protestant ears. Cyril explains how this bread and this wine are no longer merely *just* bread or wine any longer despite appearances.

It seems as though some doubted this or perhaps were a little sceptical, because Cyril goes on to explain that since Jesus himself declared the bread to be his body, and the wine to be his blood, "who shall dare to doubt any longer ... who shall ever hesitate, saying, that it is not His blood?".

This view was not uncommon amongst early church writers, and even today in certain branches and denominations there exists this belief, either in the form of *transubstantiation*[159] or of the *Real Presence*[160] doctrine, both diametrically opposed to the view that it is purely symbolic.

Cyril argues against the doubt by referencing the wedding at Cana and how Jesus turned water into wine by asking, "is it incredible that He should have turned wine into blood?"

The Real Presence

So then, with "full assurance" that something miraculous takes place during the Eucharist, let us partake of this most holy meal, "for in the figure of Bread is given to you His Body, and in the figure of wine His Blood" so that we may also become the "same body and the same blood with Him", since what we eat is then distributed throughout our own bodies. Cyril points to Peter's words and states that this is a way in which we become "participants of the divine nature"[161] through eating of the Body and Blood.

Emphasising the spiritual nature behind the bread

---

159 The Roman Catholic doctrine that the bread and wine, used in the Lord's Supper or Eucharist, actually become the literal body and blood of Christ at the "consecration" by the ordained priest. <http://www.theopedia.com/transubstantiation>

160 The Real Presence of Christ in the Eucharist (sometimes also known as Consubstantiation) is a term used to explain that Jesus is spiritually present in the elements, and not merely symbolically or metaphorically. <http://www.theopedia.com/consubstantiation>

161 *cf.* 2 Peter 1:4

and the wine, Cyril then points to the time when Jesus argued with the Jews over his statement that they would need to "eat the flesh of the Son of Man and drink his blood"[162] if they wanted to have eternal life in them, and how they missed the point of Jesus' words and were offended, not "having heard His saying in a spiritual sense".

This bread was also prefigured in the Old Testament, called the "show bread", or "the bread of The Presence",[163] which has now come to an end in Christ who is the *Bread of Heaven*, broken for us so that we may have true life.[164]

Spiritual Presence, Not Physical

Quoting from David in Psalm 23:5, when he says that *'the Lord prepares table before him in the presence of his enemies'*, Cyril interprets this in light of the Eucharist as meaning that before Christ came, the table was one of demons, polluted with idols and defiled by their nature. But since Jesus, that table which God prepared is that "mystical and spiritual Table" which is now contrary and in opposition to the Evil One. Before, you communed with demons, but now, with God.

Now this spiritual table is where we eat and commune with God, and though it may look like

---

162 *cf.* Jn 6:53

163 *cf.* Exodus 35:13; 39:35

164 *cf.* Jn 6:33,50-51

simple bread and wine, we take it on faith that it is more.

> Consider therefore the Bread and the Wine not as bare elements, for they are, according to the Lord's declaration, the Body and Blood of Christ; for even though sense suggests this to you, yet let faith establish you. Judge not the matter from the taste, but from faith be fully assured without misgiving, that the Body and Blood of Christ have been vouchsafed (given) to you.

Cyril then points to Solomon, saying he hinted at this grace found in the Eucharist in Ecclesiastes 9:7-8. *"Go, eat your bread with enjoyment ... Let your garments always be white"* — receive the joy that Christ gives and press on toward salvation now you have put off the old garment and are clothed with a garment which is always "spiritually white".

Cyril closes off his lecture by saying that now his new converts have "learned these things", they should be fully assured that, "the seeming bread is not bread, though sensible to taste, but the Body of Christ; and that the seeming wine is not wine, though the taste will have it so, but the Blood of Christ".

Before I began writing this book and studying the Church Fathers more, I held to a symbolic view of the Eucharist. But the more I've studied the Scriptures, alongside the Church Fathers, it has led me away from the doctrine that Communion is *purely* symbolic, and more towards the Real Presence idea that Christ is spiritually present in the elements. In many ways, I'd always leaned that way in some form, but didn't know how to verbalise it, or know what to call it, until reading more Early Church History.

To me personally, this view makes the most sense, especially when you consider the seriousness of eating the Eucharist, which Paul writes about to the Corinthian church. Otherwise why would there be such dire consequences?

> **1 Corinthians 11:27-30**
> Whoever, therefore, eats the bread or drinks the cup of the Lord in an unworthy manner will be answerable for the body and blood of the Lord. Examine yourselves, and only then eat of the bread and drink of the cup. For all who eat and drink without discerning the body, eat and drink judgement against themselves. For this reason many of you are weak and ill, and some have died.

It's definitely something worth considering and praying on if you've never heard of this view before now, especially since this was the position of the Church for hundreds of years before *Memorialism*[165] came along during the Reformation[166] — mainly through the teaching of Huldrych Zwingli[167] — though there are

---

165 The belief and doctrine that the bread and wine are purely symbolic and are taken in memory of Christ only (derived from Luke 22:19).

166 The Protestant Reformation, which began in the 16th century.

167 An early Reformed theologian (1484 – 1531), leader of the Reformation in Switzerland.

still some Protestant denominations that teach and believe in the Real Presence (such as Lutherans, Anglicans and Methodists, for example).

With this view in mind, it has definitely changed my approach and thinking towards taking the bread and wine when I'm at church, and given the whole process a lot more meaning and weight. I pray that you will also be impacted by Christ's presence and reality each and every time you partake in the divine mystery of the Eucharist. Amen.

Notes

Notes

DAY 34

CYRIL OF JERUSALEM: CATECHETICAL LECTURES: LECTURE XXIII

Today's final lecture on the mysteries by Cyril, is on the Sacred Liturgy and Communion and is an exposition based on 1 Peter 2:1.

1 Peter 2:1
Rid yourselves, therefore, of all malice, and all guile, insincerity, envy, and all slander.

Any of my liturgical readers may enjoy this one today. Cyril gives us a breakdown of the liturgy spoken in the church service when they are about to receive communion. I couldn't help but get a *little* excited when I read this lecture as it reminded me so much of my Anglican upbringing: the liturgy used in some parts, is *word-for-word*, which just goes to show how well preserved this has been down through the centuries.

For example, in the Anglican order of service, the *Liturgy of the Sacrament*[168] has these phrases:

The Lord be with you
and also with you

Lift up your hearts.
We lift them to the Lord.

Let us give thanks to the Lord our God.
It is right to give thanks and praise.

_____

168 Liturgy of the Sacrament, see: *https://www.churchofeng-land.org/prayer-and-worship/worship-texts-and-resources/common-worship/holy-communion#p175* [Accessed 30 Nov. 2017].

Holy, holy, holy Lord …

These are word-for-word what Cyril writes about when explaining the way in which a church service is conducted. The only difference, other than different wording elsewhere, is that the Anglican service begins with the 'sign of the peace' as a handshake between members of the congregation, whereas the ancient Church was instructed to greet one another with a kiss, as Paul instructed in 1 Corinthians 16:20 (and various other places); and Peter also, in 1 Peter 5:14.

Greet One Another With A Holy Kiss

Cyril explains this is not the same as those kisses "given in public by common friends", but rather is one which "blends souls one with another, and courts entire forgiveness for them", which is a very interesting and poetic image. For men to greet one another with a kiss was a typical custom in the ancient western Mediterranean. Later in time in our culture a handshake became customary to greet people with, so it makes sense that the the sign of the peace shifted away from a kiss, though some Church branches[169] do still greet one another this way.

Each phrase of the liturgy is broken down by Cyril, and explained in more detail about why we say these

---

169 The Eastern Orthodox clergy greet one another with a holy kiss, along with some Protestant and Reformed churches as well.

things. Mostly it is self-explanatory and about focussing our hearts and minds on God while we enter into worship, as well as joining in with the angels above by reciting the hymn of the Seraphim seen in Isaiah 6:3, "so we may be partakers with the hosts of the world above in their Hymn of praise".

Prayers And Intercessions

The next order of service is the prayers to "commemorate also those who have fallen asleep before us" — but what's interesting here is the implication that it's not just in remembrance of the faithful who had died before them, either long ago as with the Prophets and Apostles, or for those in "who in past years have fallen asleep among us", but that "at *their prayers* and intercessions God would receive our petition" (emphasis mine).

Here's an early example of praying to the "saints", or rather not *to* them but with the assumption that they are already praying for us on our behalf, as they are commemorated by the prayers of the Church. Cyril goes on to say that this practice "will be a very great benefit to the souls, for whom the supplication is put up" if they have departed life with or without sin. He then offers an illustration about God to emphasise his point, using a king who is offended and banishes the one who offended him. Then if the friends of that person "should weave a crown and offer it to [the king] on behalf of those under punishment", wouldn't he then rescind the punishment?

But instead of offering up a crown, the Church "offer up Christ sacrificed for our sins, propitiating our merciful God for them as well as for ourselves", Cyril states. Prayers on behalf of the dead may seem strange to Protestant ears, though there are some *potential* passages of Scripture about this in the New Testament, albeit debated, such as 2 Tim 1:16-18 which seems to imply Onesiphorus was dead, yet Paul prays on his behalf — plus the strange reference to baptism of the dead in 1 Corinthians 15:29. Prayers for the dead was not an uncommon practice in the early centuries of the Church, though I'm not entirely sure where the practice arose initially. It has possible origins from interpreting Luke 20:38 in an open-ended way to mean the dead in Christ are alive and in communion with Him on our behalf (along with the Hebrews 12:1 *"great cloud of witnesses"* who surround us).

Luke 20:38
Now he is God not of the dead, but of the living; for to him all of them are alive.

Wherever, or however, the it began, the fact remains that prayers for/with the dead in Christ has been practised in the Church for millennia.

Cyril then moves onto the Lord's Prayer, and proceeds to break it down line by line. I won't go into that all here for the sake of space, but you can read the full text by Cyril in the companion book. After the prayer is said, they may all go and receive the Eucharist.

There's another odd thing mentioned here to do with the Eucharist, and that is that after the wine has been taken, "while the moisture is still upon thy lips, touch it with thine hands, and hallow thine eyes and brow and the other organs of sense". There's no real explanation for this practice here though, or why it should be done.

Closing off this final lecture, Cyril offers some encouragement and a form of doxology which I will quote here to end with because I think it's worth being read in full to end this part of the series:

> Hold fast these traditions undefiled and, keep yourselves free from offence. Sever not yourselves from the Communion; deprive not yourselves, through the pollution of sins, of these Holy and Spiritual Mysteries. And the God of peace sanctify you wholly; and may your spirit, and soul, and body be preserved entire without blame at the coming of our Lord Jesus Christ:--To whom be glory and honour and might, with the Father and the Holy Spirit, now and ever, and world without end. Amen

Notes

DAY 35

AMBROSE OF MILAN: CONCERNING THE MYSTERIES, CHAPS. 1–4

Who: Bishop of Milan from 374 to 397; born around 340, at Trier, Arles, or Lyons; died 4 April, 397. He was one of the most well known and respected Fathers and Doctors[170] of the Church.

What: The treatise was composed for use during the latter part of Lent, for the benefit of those about to be baptised, explaining the rites and meaning of that Sacrament, as well as Confirmation and the Holy Eucharist. All these matters were treated with the greatest respect and were set aside in the Early Church, for fear of being misused by unbelievers.

Why: Ambrose states that after the explanations he has already given of holy living (*in previous texts/lectures not included in this book*), he will now explain the 'Mysteries'. Then after giving his reasons for not having done so before, he explains the mystery of the opening of the ears, and shows how this was done by Christ Himself in times of old.

When: About 387 AD

---

170 This was a title given to certain people on account of the great advantage the whole Church has obtained from their doctrine.

This is another similar lecture to the catechisms we read over the last few days from Cyril of Jerusalem, except these are by Ambrose, the Bishop of Milan. Taught during the season of Lent, the latter part of the 40 days is when the mysteries were explained. It was only *after* baptism that it was considered the acceptable time to teach these things though, otherwise it was thought to have "betrayed … the Mysteries" rather than portray them properly.

> Open, then, your ears, inhale the good savour of eternal life which has been breathed upon you by the grace of the sacraments

After the deacons have said the above, the following words were then declared over the catechumens:[171] *"Epphatha, which is, Be opened"*.[172]

Similar to what Cyril taught, the new converts renounced the devil by facing West, and then turning East towards Christ, as though face to face, they declared their acceptance of Him. The bishop gives a message or blessing to the convert, who is instructed to acknowledge him as though he were an angel of the Lord, and to not pay attention to his outward appearance as a man, but to respect the Office he holds

171 "Catechumen," in the early Church, was the name applied to those who had not yet been initiated into the "sacred mysteries", but was undergoing a teaching course for that purpose. The word comes from the Greek κατηχέω (katécheó), meaning "teach" or "instruct", found in Gal 6:6. *cf. https://www.biblestudytools.com/dictionary/catechist-catechumen/*

172 *cf.* Mark 7:34

as an authority.

God's Presence In Baptism

"What did you see?", Ambrose rhetorically asks about the baptism. Water, of course, but not only that: apart from the bishop and deacons ministering during this time, God is also present in the waters. Quoting Paul from 2 Corinthians 4:18, he makes the point that there are "things which are not seen" along with the "the invisible things of God"[173] at work here, and if they should accept and believe the working of the Spirit during baptism, then why not the presence also, for one always precedes the other, Ambrose says.

Using the story of Naaman,[174] amongst others from the Old Testament, Ambrose makes a comparison to show how baptism was prefigured in various places throughout the Scriptures. On visiting the prophet and being told to dip in the river to cure his leprosy, Naaman refused at first until eventually he went ahead with and did it; and on coming up out of the waters cleansed and healed, he "understood that it is not of the waters but of grace that a man is cleansed" — something which Ambrose points out.

So it is with baptism; it is not the water that is anything special or "magical", but it is purely by the grace of God alone by which we are cleansed of our sins through baptism, and given a clean conscience, as

---

173 *cf.* Rom 1:20

174 *cf.* 2 Kings 5

Peter also wrote[175] in this epistle.

That Water Does Not Cleanse Without The Spirit

"For except a man be born again of water and of the Spirit, he cannot enter into the kingdom of God."[176] — Ambrose uses this to make the point that without water, the "Sacrament of Regeneration" is of no effect, so he urges the catechumens to believe "that these waters are not void of power"!

Encouraging words, with an interesting and insightful look at the early beliefs and teaching on baptism. We'll read the conclusion of this treatise by Ambrose tomorrow.

---

175 *cf.* 1 Peter 3:21

176 *cf.* John 3:5

Notes

Notes

DAY 36

AMBROSE OF MILAN: CONCERNING THE MYSTERIES, CHAPS. 5-9

Continuing on from yesterday, we'll jump straight into the second, and final part, of Ambrose's short catechism on the Mysteries.

Continuing on the mystery of baptism, Ambrose explains that Christ is Himself present in Baptism, and because of that we shouldn't consider the person who is doing the baptising, since spiritually it is Christ himself baptising us. He then goes on to give a brief explanation of the confession of the Trinity, which is usually said by those being baptised, and how confessing belief in Father, Son and Spirit doesn't mean accepting one more than the other, but that they are all equal.

One thing of importance they must also confess is "the cross of the Lord Jesus alone". Ambrose gives no additional explanation to this, but I suppose it just means that they accept the Gospel and reject all other religions and beliefs that they may have had.

Fire From Heaven

Ambrose also makes a link between a couple of times in the Old Testament where a sacrifice was consumed with heavenly fire, and the baptism of fire we receive in the New Testament.

In Judges 6:21 when Jerubbaal had an angel burn up the sacrifice, and another time in 1 Kings 18:38 when Elijah was battling with the prophets of Baal, fire from the Lord came down to burn it up. "To those [of old] a visible fire was sent that they might believe; for us who believe, the Lord works invisibly" — our fire from heaven is in the form of the Spirit of God who falls upon us; we who are "living sacrifices" to the Lord Jesus.[177]

Anointed As Priests

After baptism, straight from coming out of the water, the catechumens are then anointed with oil.

This isn't a small dab of oil wiped on the forehead, but it is poured over their heads to run down through their beards, just as David wrote about Aaron in Psalm 133:2. This is so that they, like the Israelites, "may become a chosen race, priestly and precious, for we are all anointed with spiritual grace for a share in the Kingdom of God and in the priesthood".[178]

Ambrose points out here something unusual I've not heard before about foot washing. After the baptising and anointing with oil, the converts then have their feet washed because of the example set by Jesus. It really is an example we are meant to follow too which is something I hadn't noticed before, nor ever really been taught. Jesus specifically said to his disciples:

John 13:14-15
So if I, your Lord and Teacher, have washed your feet,

---

177 *cf.* Rom 12:1

178 *cf.* 1 Peter 2:9

you also ought to wash one another's feet. For I have set you an example, that you also should do as I have done to you.

Ambrose interprets this as meaning that although Peter was clean (vv.13),

> ...his feet were therefore washed, that hereditary sins might be done away, for our own sins are remitted through baptism [...] since the Author of Salvation Himself redeemed us through His obedience, how much more ought we His servants to offer the service of our humility and obedience.

After all of this process is done, the catechumens are then given a white robe to wear to symbolise the putting off of sins and the old self, and of putting on "the chaste veil of innocence", as Isaiah prophesied: *"Though your sins be as scarlet, I will make them white as snow"*.[179]

A More Excellent Sacrament

Ambrose makes a point here that even though the Jews had manna and quail sent by God, and it was physical and seen, the Church now has sacraments which "are both more ancient than those of the synagogue, and more excellent than the manna" because "no eye has seen, nor ear heard, nor the human heart conceived,

---

179 *cf.* Isaiah 1:18

what God has prepared for those who love him",[180] for the invisible things of God cannot be comprehended by the human mind.

As "water flowed from the rock" for the people of old,[181] Ambrose says, now "for you Blood flowed from Christ" — that water only satisfied them for a short time, but now the Blood of Christ satisfies us for all eternity; just as the Body of Christ is now far better than the manna, "for light is better than shadow" which these things prefigured.

Ambrose finishes of his lecture with a lengthy explanation about the Eucharist and how it really is the body and blood of Christ, even though it may still look like bread and wine. He goes on to give many examples from the Old Testament about how the prophets did many things contrary to nature, such as the axe head floating,[182] the Red Sea parting,[183] etc., so why now is it so hard to believe that by blessing and consecration, the bread and wine change their nature to become the true Body and Blood? He makes a valid point — these things aren't called "mysteries" for no reason.

After saying this, he then goes on to say that if these elements can be changed in nature, then so are we by being born again through the waters of baptism, even

---

180 *cf.* 1 Cor 2:9

181 *cf.* Num 20:11

182 *cf.* 2 Kings 6:1-7

183 *cf.* Exodus 14:21

though we don't re-enter the womb to be physically changed. The Spirit is working in us and through us to make the change, just as He does in the elements of the Eucharist.

Something that has become clearer each day we read these types of early letters and lectures, is that the early church accepted some form of Real Presence[184] or transubstantiation[185] in the Eucharist. I'll leave it up to you to decide whether or not you can accept this, if you don't already. Personally, it has challenged me to reconsider my beliefs on the Eucharist.

I'll instead close off with this quote from Ambrose, because whatever we believe concerning these things, we truly are sealed by the Spirit of God first, and our understanding of doctrine comes second:

> So that the Lord Jesus Himself, invited by such eager love and by the beauty of comeliness and grace, since now no offenses pollute the baptized, says to the Church: *"Place Me as a seal upon your heart, as a signet upon your arm"*[186]

---

184 The Real Presence of Christ in the Eucharist (sometimes also known as Consubstantiation) is a term used to explain that Jesus is spiritually present in the elements, and not merely symbolically or metaphorically. <http://www.theopedia.com/consubstantiation>

185 The Roman Catholic doctrine that the bread and wine, used in the Lord's Supper or Eucharist, actually become the literal body and blood of Christ at the "consecration" by the ordained priest. <http://www.theopedia.com/transubstantiation>

186 *cf.* Song of Songs 8:6

Notes

DAY 37

LEO THE GREAT: LETTER XXVIII (CALLED THE "TOME")

Who: Leo the Great, also known as Pope St. Leo I (the Great), was Pope from 440-461 AD. His place and date of birth are unknown; died 10 November, 461. Leo's pontificate,[187] next to that of St. Gregory I, is the most significant and important in Christian antiquity, as he tried to combat the heresies which seriously threatened church unity even in the West, such as Pelagianism.[188]

What: A defence of the twofold nativity and nature of Christ against the false teaching of a priest called Eutyches. It is a doctrinal letter, often referred to as "The Tome", sent by Pope Leo I in the year 449 to Flavian, Patriarch of Constantinople, on the Church's teaching about the person of Christ.

Why: An apologetic[189] defending the faith to ensure sound teaching is passed on and understood by all to affirm that Christ has two natures, human and divine, united in the one divine Person of the Son of God.

When: 3 June, 449 AD

---

187 The office or term of office of a pontiff (Pope).

188 Pelagianism derives its name from Pelagius, who lived in the 5th century A.D.. The doctrine denied original sin as well as Christian grace. See: *https://carm.org/pelagianism*

189 A formal defence or justification of a theory or doctrine.

Today's reading is a defence of the faith against certain things that a priest called Eutyches was teaching, written by Pope Leo I.

Eutyches was speaking against the teaching of the Archbishop of Constantinople, Nestorius, who said that the human experiences of Christ were only part of the 'the man' which was distinct from the 'God the Word' part of Jesus. To combat this, Eutyches went too far in the other direction and declared that Christ was "a fusion of human and divine elements" which created a new, single nature in Jesus, rather than a twofold nature which the Creeds declare. This actually led to himself being declared a heretic also for this belief![190]

Now Leo comes into this and begins writing against the teaching of Eutyches because it seems that he was unwilling to accept any correction to his doctrine. "But what more iniquitous", Leo says, "than to hold blasphemous opinions, and not to give way to those who are wiser and more learned than ourself?"

Leo is quite scathing actually, and doesn't hold back on denouncing the man or his teaching:

> Now into this unwisdom fall they who, finding themselves hindered from knowing the truth by some obscurity … thus they stand out as masters of error because they were never disciples of truth...

---

190 This heresy is known as *Eutychianism,* and was declared as such by the Council of Chalcedon in 451 AD.

He goes on to wonder how Eutyches could not have been corrected by others or by more in-depth study; or even *want* to change his view when even the the Creeds say otherwise, which is the measure by which all heresies are defeated.

> [Has he] not even grasped the rudiments of the Creed? And that which, throughout the world, is professed by the mouth of everyone who is to be born again … By which ... the devices of almost all heretics are overthrown.

The Creed

He goes on to quote the statements of the Creed, which is confessed by all of the Churches as the commonly accepted as the fundamentals of the faith, to make his point and contrast with what Eutyches said and taught:

> He is God from God, Almighty from Almighty, and being born from the Eternal one is co-eternal with Him; not later in point of time, not lower in power, not unlike in glory, not divided in essence: but at the same time the only begotten of the eternal Father was born eternal of the Holy Spirit and the Virgin Mary.

Leo goes through many instances in the New Testament, from the Gospels to Paul's letters, to Old Testament prophecies, to really point out that Jesus was the Word made flesh — and truly flesh, not some deception.

If Eutyches had read all these things closely, "then he would not speak so erroneously as to say that the Word became flesh in such a way that Christ, born of the Virgin's womb, had the form of man, but had not the reality of His mother's body", Leo states.

What Eutyches was teaching sounds a lot like Docetism,[191] the heresy which was around more prominently a couple of centuries earlier.

Instead, and in contrast to this, the commonly accepted doctrine on the nature of Jesus is explained by Leo as being, "without detriment therefore to the properties of either nature and substance which then came together in one person, majesty took on humility, strength weakness, eternity mortality...". In theological terms, this concept of Jesus having two natures in one body has come to be known as the *hypostatic union*[192]. Leo maintains that Jesus Christ is one person of the Trinity who has two distinct natures which are permanently united together.

Leo's Tome was later recognized by the Council of Chalcedon[193] (451 AD) as a statement of orthodox Christology, which gave rise to the Chalcedonian

---

191 Docetism was an error concerning the nature of Christ. It taught that Jesus only *appeared* to have a body and that he wasn't really physically incarnate. This was also condemned at the Council of Chalcedon in 451 AD. See: *https://carm.org/docetism*

192 Also known as "the two natures of Jesus". It is the doctrine that states that Jesus as a singular person has two distinct natures: human and divine, so that he is truly man and truly God.

Creed[194] specifically for teaching and formalising this doctrine on Christ's nature.

Chalcedonian Creed

Because of the historical significance, I'm going to quote the whole of the Creed here since it is a result of Leo's work:

> We, then, following the holy Fathers, all with one consent, teach men to confess one and the same Son, our Lord Jesus Christ, the same perfect in Godhead and also perfect in manhood; truly God and truly man, of a reasonable soul and body; consubstantial with us according to the manhood; in all things like unto us, without sin; begotten before all ages of the Father according to the Godhead, and in these latter days, for us and for our salvation, born of the virgin Mary, the mother of God, according to the manhood; one and the same Christ, Son, Lord, Only-begotten, to be acknowledged in two natures, inconfusedly, unchangeably, indivisibly, inseparably; the distinction of natures being by no means taken away by the union, but rather the property of each nature being preserved, and concurring in one Person and one Subsistence, not parted or divided into two persons, but one and the

193 The Council of Chalcedon was an ecumenical council that took place from October 8 – November 1, 451 A.D at Chalcedon, a city in Asia Minor. It is the fourth of the first seven Ecumenical Councils in Christianity. *cf.* Fred Sanders and Klaus Issler, eds., *Jesus in Trinitarian Perspective: An Introductory Christology* (Nashville: B&H, 2007), p. 23.

194 The *Chalcedonian Creed* came about from Council of Chalcedon to combat heretical views about the nature of Christ. See: *http://www.theopedia.com/chalcedonian-creed*

same Son, and only begotten, God the Word, the Lord Jesus Christ, as the prophets from the beginning have declared concerning him, and the Lord Jesus Christ himself taught us, and the Creed of the holy Fathers has handed down to us.

Despite all of this correction and teaching, Eutyches kept on promoting his doctrine saying, *"I confess that our Lord had two natures before the union but after the union I confess but one"*, to which Leo responds by saying that he is "surprised that so absurd and mistaken a statement" was not picked up on by others, and that now this teaching was reaching, "the height of stupidity and blasphemy"!

Leo does end this letter on a positive note though, by saying that if Eutyches, "grieves over [his heresy] faithfully and to good purpose, and, late though it be, acknowledges how rightly the bishop's authority" is on these matters, then he can come back into the Church.

All in all, this letter is a very thorough and detailed apologetic and defence of the Faith on the nature of Christ in the incarnation, so much that I think it can still stand on it's own today without additional commentary. I'd recommend anyone interested in this topic to read Leo's Tome in full to really grasp his arguments and get a good understanding of Christ's dual nature.

Notes

Notes

DAY 38

LEO THE GREAT:
SERMON XXI
(ON THE NATIVITY FEAST I)

Who: Leo the Great, also known as Pope St. Leo I (the Great), was Pope from 440-461 AD. His place and date of birth are unknown; died 10 November, 461. Leo's pontificate,[195] next to that of St. Gregory I, is the most significant and important in Christian antiquity, as he tried to combat the heresies which seriously threatened church unity even in the West, such as Pelagianism.[196]

What: A sermon on the Nativity during Christmas time, about the incarnation of the Word of God.

Why: To explain the incarnation and preach the Good News of our Lord and Saviour becoming man for our sake, so that we may be saved and born again.

When: Between 440 and 461 AD

---

195 The office or term of office of a pontiff (Pope).

196 Pelagianism derives its name from Pelagius, who lived in the 5th century A.D.. The doctrine denied original sin as well as Christian grace. See: *https://carm.org/pelagianism*

Today's reading is a Christmas sermon from Pope Leo I. This may seem totally out of place (depending on when you read this, of course), but there is some sense and logic going on here! This reading marks the beginning of the final three days of this book, and the topics covered all work together in the build up to the glorious resurrection of Christ and serves as a great way to round off this series of readings with a walk through of the life, death and resurrection of Jesus.

This sermon reading deals with the first coming of our Lord as a baby, the mighty Word of God incarnated as a small and fragile child to save the world. Having just recently become a father myself, seeing how delicate and fragile a newborn baby really is — it just blows my mind that the Son of God stepped down from all his glory and majesty to be born into a tiny little delicate body that was totally dependant on others to keep safe and to look after!

Tomorrow's sermon goes over aspects of Lent itself, in which we celebrate and remember the life and ministry of Jesus; and then finally, the last sermon is on the resurrection where we celebrate Christ's triumph over sin and death which is what Easter is all about. So in short, these sermons cover the major points in the life of Jesus, which is quite fitting to close this series with.

Celebrating Christmas is to celebrate *"the birthday of the Life, which destroys the fear of mortality and brings to us the joy of promised eternity"*.

I really like that thought, that Christmas and the incarnation is the "birthday of life".

> There is for all one common measure of joy, because as our Lord the destroyer of sin and death finds none free from charge, so is He come to free us all.

Through his birth, Jesus has "taken on him the nature of man, thereby to reconcile it to its Author" by defeating the devil and death.[197]

And so it was, "the Word of God, Himself God, the Son of God", the one who was in the beginning *with God*; the one by which *all things came into being*,[198] came with the purpose of saving us from "eternal death" by "bending Himself to take on Him our humility".

By doing this, the Word did not "decrease in His own majesty", but he remained "what He was and [assumed] what He was not". This was so that he "might unite the true form of a slave to that form in which He is equal to God the Father"; this then joined "both natures together by such a compact that the lower should not be swallowed up in its exaltation nor the higher impaired by its new associate".

Without detriment, the nature of God came together with the nature of man in one person; "inviolable nature was united with possible nature, and true God

---

197 *cf.* Gal 4:4

198 *cf.* Jn 1:1-3

and true man were combined to form one Lord".

This Lord is our Mediator between God and man[199] due to his dual nature, and because of this, he "could both die with the one and rise again with the other".

> For unless He were true God, He would not bring us a remedy, unless He were true Man, He would not give us an example.

"By the mystery of Baptism you were made the temple of the Holy Ghost", and through that act we put off the old man, and thus "obtained a share in the birth of Christ" and became "a partner in the Divine nature".[200]

So even though this was a sermon about the Nativity, it was more focused on the nature of the incarnation and how that relates to us with regards to salvation. We were purchased for a price, the "money is the blood of Christ" which brings salvation to all of the world.

Let us go forth towards the resurrection in confidence at what Christ has done for us, working out our salvation by the power of the Spirit in us, who reigns for ever and ever. Amen

---

199 *cf.* 1 Tim 2:5

200 *cf.* 2 Peter 1:4

Notes

Notes

DAY 39

LEO THE GREAT: SERMON XLIX (ON LENT XI)

Who: Leo the Great, also known as Pope St. Leo I (the Great), was Pope from 440-461 AD. His place and date of birth are unknown; died 10 November, 461. Leo's pontificate,[201] next to that of St. Gregory I, is the most significant and important in Christian antiquity, as he tried to combat the heresies which seriously threatened church unity even in the West, such as Pelagianism.[202]

What: A sermon on the season of Lent as the Easter festival approached.

Why: To encourage the Church to fast during this season in order than they may put away temptations and overcome their vices and to be guided by God in all things.

When: Between 440 and 461 AD

---

201 The office or term of office of a pontiff (Pope).

202 Pelagianism derives its name from Pelagius, who lived in the 5th century A.D.. The doctrine denied original sin as well as Christian grace. See: *https://carm.org/pelagianism*

Today's reading is a Lenten sermon from Pope Leo I that he preached in the run up to the Easter festival,[203] in which "the greatest and most binding of fasts is kept, and its observance is imposed on all the faithful without exception; because no one is so holy that he ought not to be holier, nor so devout that he might not be devouter."

Lent is a time of self-reflection and discipline, a time where we look at the life of Jesus and mourn his death, as the disciples did, before we realise the reality of the resurrection which comes a few short days later.

"Who is there who would not wish for additions to his virtue, or removal of his vice?" Leo asks rhetorically, referring to the benefits of the Lenten fast and discipline.

"Blessed, therefore, is the mind that passes the time of its pilgrimage in chaste sobriety, and loiters not in the things through which it has to walk". Leo refers this back to what Paul taught in 1 Corinthians 7:29-31 as living in such a way that we don't get too caught up in this life and this world that we forget about the divine promise and the life we are called to live.

In a similar vein, Leo speaks about the broad and narrow paths that Jesus taught about in Matthew 7:14.

---

203 Easter was celebrated with a feast like Passover among the early churches. For a short summary of early Christian worship practices, see:
http://www.christianitytoday.com/history/issues/issue-37/worship-in-early-church-did-you-know.html

He says that the broad path is crowded with those who were caught up with this life and who followed their own desires over the Lord, despite "that which [the flesh] desires [being] short-lived and uncertain, yet men endure toil more willingly for the lust of pleasure than for love of virtue", which leads to the why the wide road is filled with unnumbered people who chase after the visible. But the narrow path, for those who prefer the eternal, unseen things, is few and far between for those seeking salvation.[204]

Satan Robbed Of All His Tyrannical Power

It is during this season, Leo goes on to say, that Satan is "consumed with the strongest jealousy and now tortured with the greatest vexation" due to the great number of people fasting to renew their faith and discipline in following Christ. Even those who had slipped into worldly cares, became lukewarm or were just weak in faith, "furnished [themselves] with spiritual armour" and renewed their enthusiasm!

Through Jesus' victory on the cross, many people turned to faith, and so Satan was "driven from the hearts of those he once possessed" and was stripped of his power over such people. But as James wrote, "all of us make many mistakes",[205] so we must all be willing to forgive one another, in order that we don't violate the holy command in the Lord's prayer which

204 *cf.* 2 Cor 4:18; Rom 8:24

205 *cf.* James 3:2

we bind ourselves to, where it says, *"forgive those who sin against us"*.[206] He says this because it is often during this time that Satan brings temptations or divisions amongst the Church to cause us to sin and make mistakes.

Our Duties During Lent

Leo goes on to say that we must strive to be peacemakers because they will be blessed and "called children of God",[207] so especially now, any discord or enmity between other believers should be rectified and reconciled; otherwise, "let no one think to have a share in the Paschal feast[208] that has neglected to restore brotherly peace"!

Aside from forgiveness and reconciliation amongst ourselves, Leo also says that our fast-times should be "fat and abound" with regards to almsgiving and care of the poor.

"Let each bestow on the weak and destitute those dainties which he denies himself", Leo says, which is reminiscent of other ancient sources which say similar things with regards to fasting, and to giving to the poor whatever you didn't use for yourself that day.[209]

206 *cf.* Luke 11:4

207 *cf.* Matt 5:9

208 Another name for the Easter feast/Passover.

209 The Shepherd of Hermas (~140 AD) says: "... and having reckoned up the price of the dishes of that day which you intended to have eaten, you will give it to a widow, or an orphan, or to some person in want …" (*Herm.* Similitude 5:3*).*

Leo ends this sermon with an interesting view on forgiveness of sins being tied to baptism, repentance and *almsgiving*, and also quotes *Sirach 3:30* as Scripture to back up his point: *"As water extinguishes a blazing fire, so almsgiving atones for sin"*.

Regardless of that, it is right to focus on helping the poor and destitute during our times of fasting, which is the true fast which the Lord wants from us, as he said through the prophet Isaiah:

Isaiah 58:6-7
Is not this the fast that I choose:
  to loose the bonds of injustice,
  to undo the thongs of the yoke,
  to let the oppressed go free,
and to break every yoke?

Is it not to share your bread with the hungry,
and bring the homeless poor into your house;
when you see the naked, to cover them,
and not to hide yourself from your own kin?

Let us bear this in mind always, not only during the season of Lent, but in every situation we encounter. Amen.

Notes

DAY 40

LEO THE GREAT: SERMON LXXII (ON THE LORD'S RESURRECTION, II)

Who: Leo the Great, also known as Pope St. Leo I (the Great), was Pope from 440-61 AD. Place and date of birth unknown; died 10 November, 461. Leo's pontificate[210], next to that of St. Gregory I, is the most significant and important in Christian antiquity, as he tried to combat the heresies which seriously threatened church unity even in the West, such as Pelagianism[211].

What: A sermon on the Gospel, incarnation and resurrection of our Lord.

Why: To encourage the Church in the power of the incarnation and the true faith and the nature of Christ and to give a new meaning to Passover in light of Jesus.

When: Between 440 and 461 AD

---

210 The office or term of office of a pontiff (Pope).

211 Pelagianism derives its name from Pelagius, who lived in the 5th century A.D.. The doctrine denied original sin as well as Christian grace. See: *https://carm.org/pelagianism*

Here we are at the final day of this series. I hope you've found it an interesting journey through Church History, covering various authors and topics from the first four centuries of the Church. And what better way to end this series than with a sermon on the **resurrection!**

"The whole of the Easter mystery, dearly-beloved, has been brought before us in the Gospel narrative", Leo declares as the opening statement of this sermon.

What is this Easter mystery? "The cross of Christ, which was set up for the salvation of mortals" which is both a "mystery and an example" for us to follow. It's "a sacrament where by the Divine power takes effect" and "an example whereby man's devotion is excited" to be "inseparably united to" Christ — he who is "*the Way* that is of holy living, *the Truth* of Divine doctrine, and *the Life* of eternal happiness.[212]

Christ Took Our Nature Upon Him For Our Salvation

In the beginning, when the "whole body of mankind had fallen", our merciful God had purposed in himself to make a way to reconcile "His creatures made after His image [...] through His only-begotten Jesus Christ".

Leo goes on to say that if we had not fallen from how God made us, we'd have been happy; but now we

---

212 *cf.* Jn 14:6

can be happier if we remain in what he has remade us to be through his Spirit.

Jesus was "excluded [from] all taint of the sin which has passed upon all men", that taint being "weakness and mortality, which were not sin, but the penalty of sin". The "Redeemer of the World" suffered these things for our sake, "that they might be reckoned as the price of redemption".

In us is the "heritage of condemnation", but in Christ is the *"mystery of godliness".*[213]

Through the enemy, Jesus had "His spotless flesh" tortured, and because of this, Jesus willingly went to die for us. Now "believers in Him might find neither persecution intolerable, nor death terrible, by the remembrance that there was no more doubt about their sharing His glory than there was about His sharing their nature".

Set Your Minds On Things That Are Above

Following on with the previous thought, Leo goes on to explain that, "in Christ we are crucified, we are dead, we are buried; on the very third day, too, we are raised"; which is why Paul writes to the Colossians:

Colossians 3:1-4
So if you have been raised with Christ, seek the things

---

213 *cf.* 1 Tim 3:16

that are above, where Christ is, seated at the right hand of God. Set your minds on things that are above, not on things that are on earth, for you have died, and your life is hidden with Christ in God. When Christ who is your life is revealed, then you also will be revealed with him in glory.

We achieve this raising by the power of Christ with us, who lifts us up, because he is with us, as he promised: *"I am with you always, to the end of the age"*.[214] This in itself fulfils the promise that his own name means: "God with us", as prophesied by Isaiah.[215]

But even in Christ's ascending, he has not forsaken us, because even though he sits at "the right hand of God",[216] he also dwells within the whole Body of believers.[217]

"Christ's victory is assuredly ours", just as we should expect since Jesus has "conquered the world!".[218] Whatever we battle against in this world, whether lust or greed, or heresy, "let us arm ourselves always with the Lord's Cross" so that our "Paschal feast will never end" by abstaining from the "leaven of wickedness" and having the mind of Christ.[219]

---

214 *cf.* Matt 28:20

215 *cf.* Isa 7:14 — *"... shall name him Immanuel."*

216 *cf.* Acts 2:32-33

217 *cf.* Eph 1:22-23

218 *cf.* Jn 16:33

219 *cf.* 1 Cor 2:16

The Nature Of The Incarnation

For only those who hold to the correct view of the incarnation can properly appreciate Easter and the Lord's Passover, Leo says. In explaining this thought, he gives a sort of creedal statement similar to the Nicene Creed to demonstrate his beliefs on the matter:

> For the Son of God is true God, having from the Father all that the Father is, with no beginning in time, subject to no sort of change, undivided from the One God, not different from the Almighty, the eternal Only-begotten of the eternal Father; so that the faithful intellect believing in the Father and the Son and the Holy Ghost in the same essence of the one Godhead, neither divides the Unity by suggesting degrees of dignity, nor confounds the Trinity by merging the Persons in one.

When Jesus emptied himself for our sake and restoration,[220] it was not for the loss of power, but for compassion, for there is no other name under heaven by which we are saved![221] In expounding on Philippians 2, Leo draws some nice contrasts which highlight just what Jesus did when he stepped down from Heaven:

> …the Invisible made His substance visible, the Intemporal temporal, the Impassible passible: not that power might sink into weakness, but that weakness might pass into indestructible power…

---

220 *cf.* Philippians 2:5-8

221 *cf.* Acts 4:12

A New Meaning For Passover

Quoting John 13:1, Leo reinterprets Passover as now meaning that it was about the time when Jesus should "pass out of this world unto the Father". In terms of Jesus' nature during that time, he goes on to say that: "because the Word and the Flesh is one Person, the Assumed is not separated from the Assuming nature", meaning also that humanity is now forever a part of the Godhead, and therefore it promotes our nature as one which will one day be glorified in the resurrection.

Philippians 3:20-21

But our citizenship is in heaven, and it is from there that we are expecting a Saviour, the Lord Jesus Christ. He will transform the body of our humiliation that it may be conformed to the body of his glory, by the power that also enables him to make all things subject to himself.

To "share in this unspeakable gift", the Lord, ahead of his Passion prepared a "blessed *passing over* for His faithful ones", and for the whole Church who were yet to come, by his prayer in John 17:20-21 which asked for total unity with one another, and also with God, in the same way that he and the Father were one.[222]

---

222 *cf.* Jn 14:20

Only True Believers Can Keep The Easter Festival

Those who deny the true nature of the Son of God, and that he is also True God, can have no part in this divine union nor in the Easter Festival. True Christians, accepting the Creed and the deity of Christ, "rightly exult and devoutly rejoice in this sacred season" of Lent and Easter (or *Pascha*[223]), and "have no doubt about Christ's Birth according to the flesh, His Passion and Death, and the Resurrection of His body … who was truly born of a Virgin's womb, truly hung on the wood of the cross, truly laid in an earthly tomb, truly raised in glory, truly set on the right hand of the Father's majesty"!

This, again, is another example of a creedal statement about Jesus, much like those we saw in the the earlier texts from the first couple of centuries which sought to deal with Docetism. It really just hammers home the point of Christ's reality and life — something we should never forget.

---

223 *Pascha* comes from both the Greek and Latin words for "Easter" and was the common tern for Easter time in the early centuries.

That marks the end of this reading plan; I hope you've enjoyed it throughout these forty days and have learned something new. I pray and hope that you've had your faith built up and/or restored through reading about all the various topics, issues, doctrinal and theological statements that the Early Church went through to preserve the Faith, despite all of the persecution along the way!

But if nothing else, remember always: **HE IS RISEN!**

Amen.

__Notes__

Notes

ABOUT THE AUTHOR

Luke has a BA (hons) in *Biblical Studies and Theology* and has been reading and studying the works of the Early Church Fathers for over five years.
After being involved in various short-term missions to South Africa, he currently lives in Devon, England, where he co-founded WebBoss Ltd, a web development software company, with his dad, Kevin.

When not working, Luke writes frequently on his theological blog, *That Ancient Faith,* or spends time with his wife Lucy and his new daughter, Amelia.

To get in touch, or to find our more about Luke, visit:

www.fortydays.co.uk
or
www.thatancientfaith.uk

If you enjoyed this book, then please consider leaving a review online and recommending it to your friends.

Do you want to be more involved and get some behind the scenes updates, freebies and previews of new books? Then support Luke via Patreon:

https://www.patreon.com/LukeJWilson

ACKNOWLEDGEMENTS

Thanks to Jonathan Bennett and Chad Toney of *www.churchyear.net* for taking the time to create the original PDF Lenten reading plan outline which my original blog series followed.

APPENDIX A

KNOW YOUR HERESIES

What is *heresy*?

Simply put, heresy is a false teaching. It is a belief, or doctrine that is in contradiction to the accepted orthodoxy[224] of the Church.

The word "heresy" comes from the Greek[225] 'hairesis' (αἵρεσις), pronounced *hah'-ee-res-is,* which means "choosing", "sect" or "factions".

> **1 Corinthians 11:19**
> Indeed, there have to be factions among you, for only so will it become clear who among you are genuine.

Examples of heresy would be a denial of the resurrection of Christ, a teaching that salvation is obtained by works, denial that Jesus came in the flesh etc., much of which we have seen dealt with at length by various Church Fathers. Examples of modern day heresies would be Mormonism and Jehovah's Witnesses; the former teaching that people can attain godhood, the latter denying the deity of Christ (modern-day Arians).

---

224 Authorized or generally accepted theory, doctrine, or practice.
225 Strong's Concordance, *http://biblehub.com/greek/139.htm*

Below is a list of some of the major heresies which have cropped up throughout the history of the Church, each with a brief summary of what they entailed. Some of these ancient heresies still can be seen today in various forms if you know what to look for, sometimes without people realising they are verging on teaching heresy. This is why it is important to know your history so that you don't fall into error.[226]

Adoptionism — Second century: God granted Jesus supernatural powers and then adopted him as his Son at his baptism. Condemned by Pope Victor (190-198AD).

Albigenses — Middle Ages: This error taught that there were two gods: the good god of light being Jesus in the New Testament and the god of darkness and evil, or the "God of the Old Testament", being Satan. They considered the material world as evil, including the body, and thus denied the resurrection. Pope Innocent III persecuted the movement into extinction around 1208 AD.

Apollinarianism — Fourth Century: Taught by Apollinaris the Younger, bishop of Laodicea in Syria. He said that the two natures of Christ could not exist in the same person, and so taught that the mind of Jesus was *the Logos,* and the human body was a glorified version of itself, denying the true humanity of in the incarnation. Condemned by the Second General

226 For a more in-depth look at heresy, see:
   https://carm.org/what-is-heresy

Council at Constantinople in 381 AD.

Arianism — Fourth Century: A doctrine about Christ which taught that Jesus was created by God and was not eternal like the Father. Condemned by the Council of Nicaea in 325 AD.

Docetism — Second Century: A doctrine which taught that Jesus only *seemed* to be human, denying the incarnation and leading to a view that matter is evil. Condemned at the Council of Chalcedon in 451 AD.

Donatism — Fourth Century: A teaching that the validity of sacraments depends on the moral character of the minister. Eg. If the one performing a baptism were in sin, then the baptism would be invalid. This sect persisted for a long time and eventually died out sometime after the fifth century, with the help of Augustine of Hippo.

Gnosticism — First Century: This had lots of variations, but generally it taught you needed special knowledge for salvation, that the physical world is evil and was created by a lesser, evil god called the *demigurge*. Condemned by the Apostles (such as in 1 John) and the earliest Church Fathers.

Modalism — Third Century: Also called Sabellianism. A denial of the Trinity stating that God is one person in three *modes*,[227] rather than the Orthodox view that God

---

227 *"That's Modalism, Patrick!";* see this video for a humorous, yet comprehensive overview of heresies related to the Trinity by Lutheran Satire: https://youtu.be/KQLfgaUoQCw

is one in three *persons.* Condemned by Dionysius, bishop of Rome around 262 AD.

Monarchism/Monarchianism — Second Century: Similar to Modalism, it taught that God is one single person, Jesus was just a man and that the Holy Spirit is a "force" or "presence" of the Father. Modern-day sects that hold to this in some form are: Jehovah's Witnesses, Christadelphians, and Unitarians.

Monophysitism — Fourth Century: A doctrine teaching that Jesus had only *one* nature and not *two* as the Orthodox and Chalcedonian doctrine of the hypostatic union states. The Council of Chalcedon rejected this doctrine in 451 AD. Condemned at the Sixth Ecumenical Council around 680 AD.

Nestorianism — Fifth Century: A teaching that Jesus was two distinct persons, both human and divine separately instead of a unified person; and that Mary was only the mother of his human side instead of a unified nature. Condemned at the Council of Ephesus in 431 AD.

Patripassianism — Another form of Modalism. This doctrine taught that the Father was incarnated and suffered on the cross.

Pelagianism — Fifth Century: This doctrine teaches that human nature is essentially good and can, of its own free will, choose God and follow his commands without any divine aid or intervention. It is an error concerning the nature of man and sin and was opposed by Augustine of Hippo and condemned at the Council of Carthage in 418 AD. It was also condemned at nine other Councils ranging from 431 – 1618!

Socinianism — Sixteenth Century: A denial of the Trinity and a similar heresy to Arianism, viewed through the lens of the rationalism of the Italian Renaissance. This teaching denied the incarnation, deity and pre-existence of Jesus, as well as saying that God was only the Father with the Holy Spirit as the power of God. It also taught that Jesus was a deified man and so should be adored as such, but that due to this, the sacrifice on the cross wasn't efficacious for redemption and only served as an example of self-sacrifice. It still exists today in some form within the Unitarians and the Jehovah's Witnesses.

Subordinationism — Fourth Century onwards: A doctrine that essentially teaches that Jesus is less than the Father in an inferior way in terms of essence, nature and being. This isn't to be confused with Jesus being subordinate to the Father in a functional sense of submitting to him (*cf.* 1 Cor 15:28). This teaching is just another form of Arianism, which was condemned at the Council of Nicaea in 325 AD.

Tritheism — Various times throughout history: The erroneous view that the Trinity is really three separate gods, instead of one God in three persons. Often held by those who misunderstand or can't accept the Orthodox position of the Trinity. A modern-day version of this error is held by Mormons, though in a unique way. Mormons believe in many gods but focus on the three which they believe oversee the Earth. So it's a type of focussed polytheism.

As you can probably see from reading through this list, many of the heresies which emerged all have similar or common roots, and any heresies that exist today will stem from one of these major errors in some form. If you're unsure about a certain sect, teaching or denomination, just look out for any of these heretical doctrines to see if they are within the boundaries of historical Orthodoxy or not.

APPENDIX B

TIMELINE OF THE EARLY CHURCH

I thought it would be helpful to give some more historical context to the writings of the Church Fathers in relation to when the books of the New Testament were approximately written, in the order that they were written, plus any relevant major historical events that may have influenced certain texts. I'm using the earlier dating method of the New Testament books, but have included some later dates for those texts which are disputed more heavily. Having said that, all dates here are approximate and could vary by a few years either way. There has been (and still is) much debate and speculation as to exact dates of when the manuscripts were originally penned, as the dating of surviving papyrus and manuscript fragments are only from the second century onwards.

On the Early Church Texts side, I've included all of the texts from this book, plus a few other notable and important early texts which weren't included in this reading plan. As an additional point of interest, Clement, Ignatius, Polycarp and Papias were all disciples or companions of the apostle John. Irenaeus later became a disciple of Polycarp, and around 67AD Ignatius became bishop of Antioch and was appointed to the position by the apostle Peter himself. Thus these few men preserved some of the earliest links back to the *Apostolic Age* and the things which were taught to those who personally knew Jesus. There is also an ancient tradition that Ignatius was the child that Jesus held when he blessed the children (*cf.* Matthew 18:1-4).

Date of New Testament Book	Significant Historical Events	Date of Early Church Texts
	Jesus Crucified - 30-33AD	
	Pentecost and the outpouring of the Holy Spirit - 33AD	
	Stephen stoned; first martyr – approx. 34AD (*cf. Acts 7:54-8:2*)	
	Jesus converts Paul on the Damascus Road – approx. 34-36AD	
	Apostle James killed by Herod – approx. 42-44AD (*cf. Acts 12:2*)	
James (early date), 45-50 AD		
Galatians, 47-57AD		Didache (early date) - 50AD
1 Thessalonians, 51-52AD		

Date of New Testament Book	Significant Historical Events	Date of Early Church Texts
2 Thessalonians, 51-52AD		
	Nero becomes emperor of Rome - 54AD	
Gospel of Mark, 50-60AD		
Gospel of Matthew, 50-60AD		
1 Corinthians, 53-54AD		
Romans, 55-57AD		
2 Corinthians, 55-56AD		
James (late date), 60-63AD		
Gospel of Luke, 60AD		
Acts of the Apostles, 61AD		
Colossians, 61AD		
Ephesians, 61AD		
	James, brother of Jesus, martyred - 62AD	
Philippians, 62-63AD		
Philemon, 63AD		

Date of New Testament Book	Significant Historical Events	Date of Early Church Texts
1 Peter, 63-64AD		
1 Timothy, 63-66AD		
Titus, 63-66AD		
	Great Fire of Rome, Nero blames Christians - 64AD	
	Persecution by Nero begins - 64-68AD	
	Apostle Peter martyred - 64-68AD	
	Apostle Paul martyred - 67-68AD	
Hebrews, 64-68AD		
Revelation (early date), 64-68AD		
2 Peter, 66AD		
	The Great Jewish Revolt against Rome - 66-73AD	
2 Timothy, 67AD		
Jude, 68-80AD		1 Clement, 69-95AD

Date of New Testament Book	Significant Historical Events	Date of Early Church Texts
	Siege of Jerusalem - 70AD	Didache, 70-100AD
	Temple Destroyed - 70AD	Epistle of Barnabas, 70-79AD
Gospel of John, 85-90AD		
1, 2 & 3 John, 85-90AD		
	Persecution by Emperor Domitian - 89-96AD	
Revelation (late date), 95-96AD		Papias of Hierapolis, Expositions of the Lord, 95-120AD
	Apostle John dies of old age – approx. 90-100AD	2 Clement, c.100AD
		Epistles of Ignatius of Antioch, 107-108AD
	Persecution by Emperor Trajan - 109-111AD	Polycarp: to the Philippians, 110-140AD
		Mathetes to Diognetus, 130-250AD

Date of New Testament Book	Significant Historical Events	Date of Early Church Texts
		The Shepherd of Hermas, 140-154AD
		Justin Martyr, First Apology, c.156AD
		Irenaeus, Against Heresies (I-V), 175-185AD
		Muratorian Canon, 180-200AD
	Persecution by Emperor Decius - 250AD	Cyprian: On The Unity Of The Church, 249-251AD
	Persecution by Emperor Valerian - 257AD	
	Persecution by Emperor Diocletian - 303AD	Eusebius, Ecclesiastical History, 300-313AD (possibly earlier)
	Christianity legalised under the Edict of Milan - 313AD	

Date of New Testament Book	Significant Historical Events	Date of Early Church Texts
		Cyril of Jerusalem: Catechetical Lectures, 348-350AD
		Athanasius: Life of Anthony, 356-362AD
		Ambrose of Milan: Concerning The Mysteries, c.387AD
		Leo the Great's Tome, 449AD
		Leo the Great, Sermons, 440-461AD

APPENDIX C

MAPS OF EARLY TEXT LOCATIONS

The next few pages contain two maps, the first lists all of the locations of the early church texts contained within this book, plus a few other notable early texts. What I have attempted to do is pinpoint where these early texts were most likely written and by whom, based on internal evidence and other sources, such as translation introductions by Schaff et al. The other map displays the journey which Ignatius took to Rome.

Alongside the early church map points, I have also listed the locations of where the New Testament epistles were sent, with a note of where they were sent from. When all of this is put together visually, I hope it will give you some real-world context of where the events and places in the New Testament and Early Church happened, as well as highlight how the early church communities formed around and near to where these apostolic churches were founded. I overlaid all of this on a map with modern-day country boundaries in order to aid with the visual context, because as helpful as displaying ancient provinces are, not everyone is as *au fait* in first century geography as others may be. So this way the intention is to enable you to easily grasp where these things took place without needing to look up additional maps just to see that ancient Galatia is now in modern-day Turkey, for example.

Locations of Early Texts

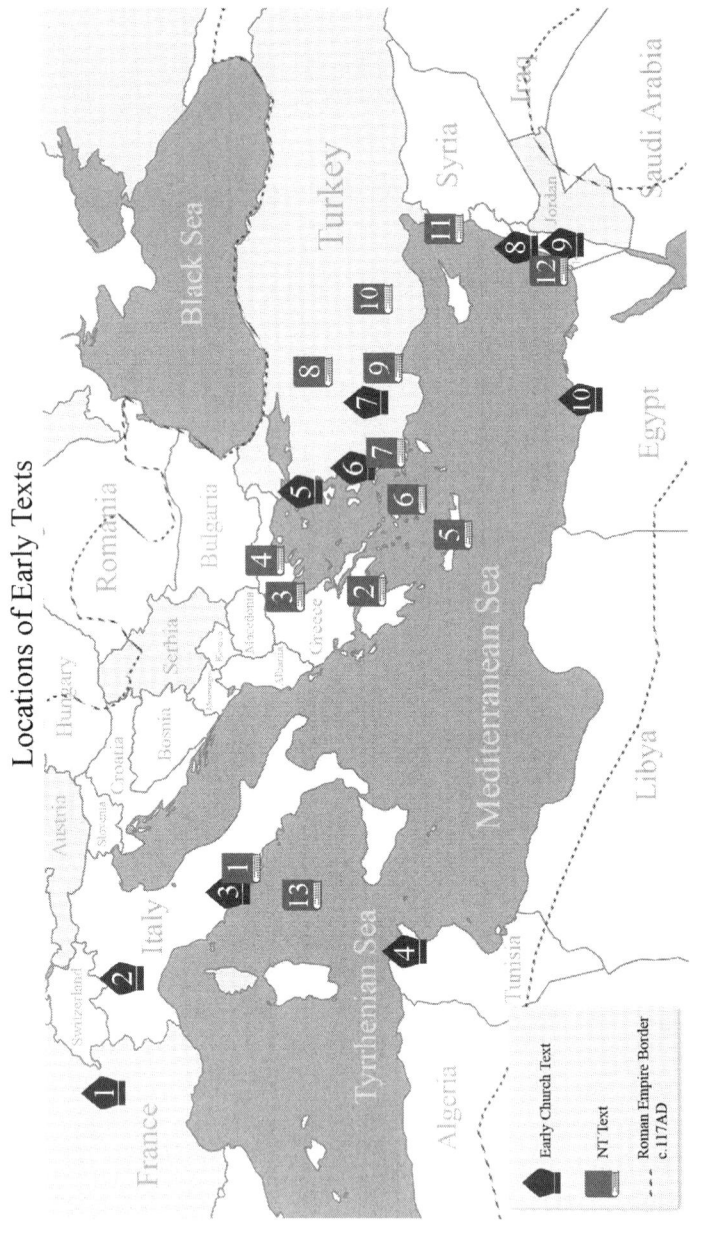

374

Map Key - Early Church Texts: Locations and Authors

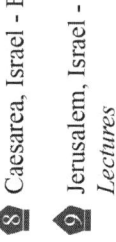

1 Lyon, France - Irenaeus, *Against Heresies*

2 Milan, Italy - Ambrose of Milan, *Concerning The Mysteries*

3 Rome, Italy -
Clement, *1 Clement* (Sent to Corinth);
The Shepherd of Hermas;
Justin Martyr, *First Apology*;
Muratorian Canon;
Leo the Great, *Collection of Sermons and Tome*

4 Carthage, Tunisia - Cyprian, *On The Unity Of The Church*

5 Alexandria Troas, Turkey - Here, Ignatius wrote to: the Philadelphians, the Smyrnaeans and to Polycarp

6 Smyrna, Turkey - Here, Ignatius wrote to: the Ephesians, the Magnesians, the Trallians and to the Romans

7 Hierapolis, Turkey - Papias was a bishop here and wrote a five book collection called, *The Exposition of the Oracles of the Lord*, which only survives in fragments today.

8 Caesarea, Israel - Eusebius, *Ecclesiastical History*

9 Jerusalem, Israel - Cyril of Jerusalem, *Catechetical Lectures*

10 Alexandria, Egypt -
Athanasius, *Life of Anthony*;
Epistle of Barnabas - Unknown, possibly Alexandria as only the Alexandrians were familiar with this letter up until the fourth century.

? Unknown -
2 Clement, Possible places of origin are Rome, Corinth, Antioch, and Alexandria;
Didache - Possibly Syria or Palestine, maybe Egypt;
Mathetes to Diognetus - Possibly in Rome or, more broadly, Italy.

Map Key - New Testament Epistles: Locations

1 Rome, Italy - Paul, *Romans* (from Corinth)

2 Corinth, Greece -
Paul, *1 Corinthians* (from Ephesus);
Paul, *2 Corinthians* (from Philippi)

3 Thessalonica, Greece -
Paul, *1 & 2 Thessalonians* (from Corinth)

4 Philippi, Greece - Paul, *Philippians* (from Rome)

5 Crete, Greece - Paul, *Titus* (from Philipi)

6 Patmos, Greece - John, *Revelation* (to the seven churches in Asia)

7 Ephesus, Turkey -
Paul, *Ephesians* (from Rome);
Paul, *1 Timothy* (from Philippi);
Paul, *2 Timothy* (from Rome)

8 Northern Turkey -
Peter, *1 Peter* (from Rome to Pontus, Galatia, Cappadocia, Asia, and Bithynia);
Peter, *2 Peter* (from Rome);
John, *1, 2 & 3 John* (from Ephesus, circular letter);

9 Colossae, Turkey -
Paul, *Colossians* (from Rome);
Paul, *Philemon* (from Rome)

10 Galatia province, Turkey - Paul, *Galatians* (from Antioch, circular letter)

11 Antioch, south-central Turkey - Jude, *Jude* (possibly from Antioch, circular letter to possibly to Syrian-Antioch audience)

12 Jerusalem, Israel - James, *James* (to the 12 tribes in the Dispersion)

13 Unknown, poss. Rome - Unknown, *Hebrews*

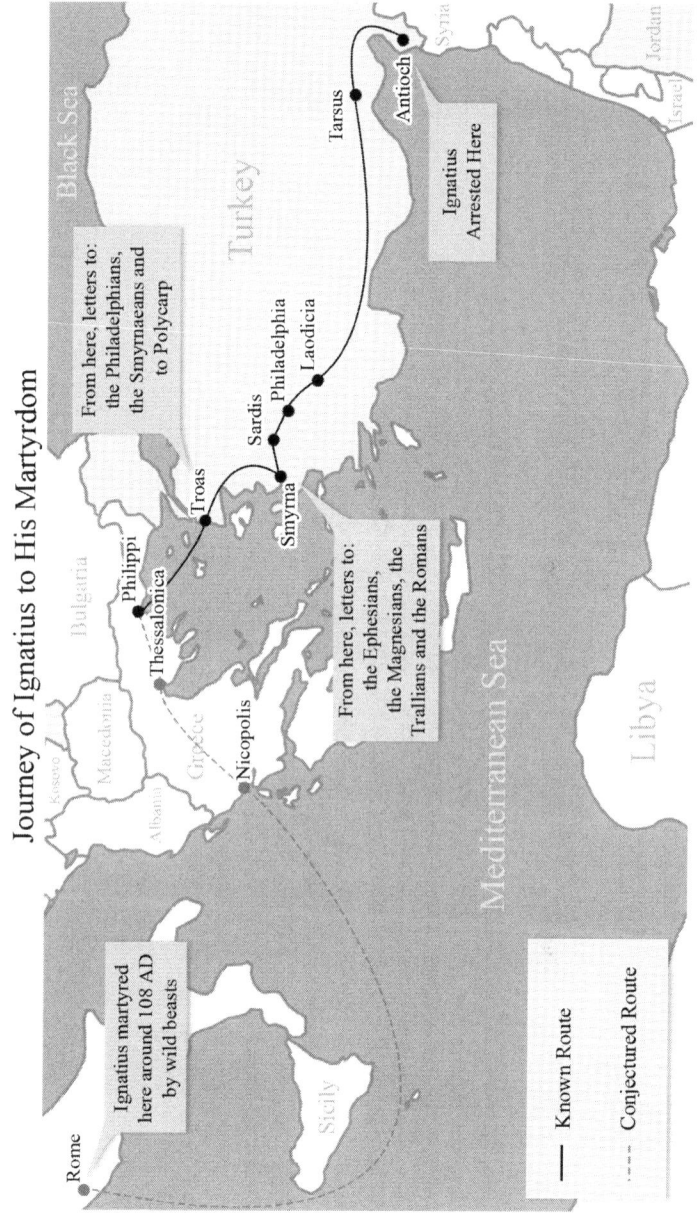

Journey of Ignatius to His Martyrdom

From here, letters to:
the Philadelphians,
the Smyrnaeans and
to Polycarp

Ignatius
Arrested Here

Ignatius martyred
here around 108 AD
by wild beasts

From here, letters to:
the Ephesians,
the Magnesians, the
Trallians and the Romans

Black Sea

Turkey

Syria

Jordan

Israel

Antioch

Tarsus

Laodicia

Philadelphia

Sardis

Smyrna

Troas

Philippi

Thessalonica

Bulgaria

Macedonia

Kosovo

Greece

Albania

Nicopolis

Mediterranean Sea

Libya

Sicily

Rome

Known Route

Conjectured Route

INDEX

Printed in Great Britain
by Amazon